Y0-CCG-358

Understanding Nursery Children

Understanding
Nursery Children

THELMA ARNOTE

Convention Press

NASHVILLE TENNESSEE

Code Number: Church Study Course
This book is number 1505 in Category 15,
Section for Adults and Young People

Library of Congress catalog card number: 63–13396
Printed in the United States of America
10. JE 63 R.R.D.

Contents

Church Study Course

THE CHURCH STUDY COURSE began October 1, 1959. It is a merger of three courses previously promoted by the Sunday School Board—the Sunday School Training Course, the Graded Training Union Study Course, and the Church Music Training Course. On October 1, 1961, the Woman's Missionary Union principles and methods studies were added.

The course is fully graded. The system of awards provides a series of five diplomas of twenty books each for Adults or Young People, two diplomas of five books each for Intermediates, and two diplomas of five books each for Juniors. Book awards earned previously in the Sunday School Training Course, the Graded Training Union Study Course, and the Church Music Training Course may be transferred to the new course.

The course is comprehensive, with books grouped into twenty categories. The purpose of the course is to help Christians to grow in knowledge and conviction, to help them to grow toward maturity in Christian character and competence for service, to encourage them to participate worthily as workers in their churches, and to develop leaders for all phases of church life and work.

The Church Study Course is promoted by the Baptist Sunday School Board, 127 Ninth Avenue, North, Nashville, Tennessee, through its Sunday School, Training Union, Church Music, and Church Administration departments; and the Woman's Missionary Union, 600 North Twentieth Street, Birmingham, Alabama; and by the respective departments in the states affiliated with the Southern Baptist Convention. A description of the course and the system of awards may be found in the leaflet "Trained Workmen," which may be obtained without charge from any one of these departments named.

A record of all awards earned should be maintained in each church. A person should be designated by the church to keep the files. Forms for such records may be ordered from any Baptist Book Store.

Requirements for Credit

IN CLASS OR HOME STUDY

IF CREDIT IS DESIRED for the study of this book in a class or by home study, the following requirements must be met:

I. IN CLASSWORK

1. The class must meet a minimum of seven and one-half clock hours. The required time does not include assembly periods. Ten class periods of forty-five minutes each are recommended. (If laboratory or clinical work is desired in specialized or technical courses, this requirement may be met by six clock hours of classwork and three clock hours of supervised laboratory or clinical work.)

2. A class member who attends all class sessions and completes the reading of the book within a week following the last class session will not be required to do any written work.

3. A class member who is absent from one or more sessions must answer the questions on all chapters he misses. In such a case, he must turn in his paper within a week, and he must certify that he has read the book.

4. The teacher should request an award for himself. A person who teaches a book in the section for Intermediates or Juniors of any category or conducts an approved unit of instruction for Nursery, Beginner, or Primary children will be granted an award in category 11, Special Studies, which will count as an elective on his own diploma. He should specify in his request the name of the book taught, or the unit conducted for Nursery, Beginner, or Primary children.

5. The teacher should complete the "Request for Book Awards —Class Study" (Form 150) and forward it within two weeks after the completion of the class to the Church Study Course Awards Office, 127 Ninth Avenue, North, Nashville 3, Tennessee.

II. IN HOME STUDY

1. A person who does not attend any class session may receive credit by answering all questions for written work as indicated in

the book. When a person turns in his paper on home study, he must certify that he has read the book.

2. Students may find profit in studying the text together, but individual papers are required. Carbon copies or duplicates in any form cannot be accepted.

3. Home study work papers may be graded by the pastor or a person designated by him or they may be sent to the Church Study Course Awards Office for grading. The form entitled "Request for Book Awards—Home Study" (Form 151) must be used in requesting awards. It should be mailed to Church Study Course Awards Office, 127 Ninth Avenue, North, Nashville 3, Tennessee.

III. CREDIT FOR THIS BOOK

This book is number 1505 in category 15, section for Adults and Young People.

About the Author

THELMA ARNOTE, a native of Missouri, attended Central Missouri State College and William Jewell College in that state. She received the B.S. and M.A. degrees from George Peabody College for Teachers in Nashville, Tennessee.

Miss Arnote, formerly the director of children's work in the Training Union Department of the Baptist Sunday School Board, Nashville, Tennessee, was also director of children's work in the First Baptist Church of Durham, North Carolina. She is presently professor of religious education and director of the Child Care Center, Southeastern Baptist Theological Seminary, Wake Forest, North Carolina.

CHAPTER 1

1

A Point of View

NO ONE CHILD or many children of any age can standard-
ize all children of a particular age. Parents say, "The
more children we have, the more sure we are that no two
are alike."

Neither is there a likelihood that any one person can
be found "understanding the Nursery child" completely.
Such a feat is not really possible for human minds. But if
one cannot achieve perfection in understanding Nursery
children, he can be introduced to them (one by one for
best results!) and perhaps enjoy a maturing friendship.

I. A PURPOSE FOR THIS WRITING

This writing is to introduce the world of children under four years of age to adults who want to know Nursery
children. It is an introduction to adults who will involve
their minds; it is an introduction to adults who will be
sensitive to words and signs. It is an invitation to think
and feel.

These are basic goals for this writing:

1. To acknowledge some apparent, inevitable facts of
growth as they seem to apply to the development of children under four years of age.

2. To inquire into the relationship between these
growth facts and children's behavior responses.

3. To raise particular questions about the meaning of
growth facts concerning the readiness of these children
for religious learning.

4. To encourage parents and friends of children to keep thinking about these ideas and to act in terms of new insights.

For what end shall persons make these mental and emotional efforts? For the end:

. . . that adults and young children may share more fully the joys each knows;

. . . that adults and young children may love one another more completely;

. . . that adults and young children may live and work together in more satisfying fellowships;

. . . that adults and young children through such community may have growing experiences with God.

II. Some Basic Ideas About Growth

People who live and work with children in quite different relationships often make similar observations. Parents, physicians, psychologists, and anthropologists may state their findings in different words, but basically, many of their observations are mutual discoveries. The strange superstitions of folklore often come close to facts in a scientific paper.

Here are some of the mutually shared ideas which appear as persons think and act and evaluate their experiences with young children. They are the basic point (or points) of view around which this book was planned.

1. *Childhood is a universal experience.*—All persons have been children. "When we try to enter a child's world we are not invading a strange land. We are homeward bound." [1] With only a little encouragement, adults are willing to recall "back when I was a child." Even though

---

[1] Arthur T. Jersild, *Child Psychology* (5th ed., Inglewood Cliffs: Prentice-Hall, Inc., 1960), p. 465.

they cannot remember much that happened to them, adults could use good memories for better understandings of early childhood. What things made me glad or sad? When was I afraid? What did I wonder about? Whom did I like? Why? The universality of childhood can be a bond of sympathetic understanding.

2. *All potentiality for growth is built-in and present at birth.*—Within six pounds of new life there are present the possibilities for all that this person can ever be or do. All potential may not be called upon, but whatever is developed in life is present in possibility at birth. The newborn infant does not speak words. Yet, unless there is physical or mental defect, he has contained within himself the possibilities for speech. In similar fashion he has present the potential for walking, running, and jumping.

3. *There is an inner urge to grow.*—Unless there is injury or malfunction, children will grow. This is the way of the human organism—to push out, to increase in size, to improve in function. In normal children there is no choice about growth. It does occur. It must happen. It is an inborn urge to completion.

4. *Growth follows inevitable patterns; it is orderly and in sequence.*—Certain things happen before other things —in all human persons. "First the blade, then the ear, after that the full corn in the ear" (Mark 4:28). This is the way of human growing and developing; it is one of the amazing examples of the dependability of creation. Taken seriously and acted upon, this fact can give great security to parents and others who seek to understand children.

All human babies must be able to raise their heads before they can lift their chests and heads off a flat surface. Similarly it is expected and counted upon that a baby will sit alone before he stands alone and stand alone before he walks alone. Such is part of the many stages in the to-be-expected sequence of walking. Likewise, not only can one always count on the fact that control of the human body proceeds from the head down (so that legs are the last to be controlled), but also one can expect that control will come from the trunk out—arms before hands, hands before fingers. In similar dependable fashion, the first tooth can be expected in the middle of the mouth!

In two- and three-year-olds the inevitable patterns persist. For the most part, early speech of toddlers consists of one-word utterances. At three, however, for many children sentences become the order of the day.

Sometimes when a parent has tried in countless ways to explain his child's behavior, he seems finally to resort to "I guess it's a stage he is going through." More often than not the parents have arrived at a basic and accurate judgment. Children will act in somewhat-to-be-expected (though not always approved) ways at particular levels of growth. In fact, if children are true to their nature, they can hardly act any other way.

5. *Though the pattern and sequence of growth are always the same, rate and speed and intensity of response vary considerably according to individuals.*—The disregard of this fact or the unwillingness to accept it causes more unhappiness, perhaps for both adults and children, than any other factor related to growth and development.

"Isn't he walking yet? Mary's baby is and she's two months younger!"

"Are you still washing diapers? I stopped that long ago!"

"I'm worried about Billy; he's six years old and has started to school, but he's not the least bit interested in reading."

Though pattern and sequence can always be counted on, rate and speed and intensity of response will vary according to individuals. Thus it is more rewarding to ask *where* the first tooth will appear rather than *when.* In acknowledgment of this growth fact, it is probably more sensible to be aware of a child's total physical response than to be concerned about his bigness or littleness.

Perhaps the greatest likeness of any human being to all other humans is that each is somehow different, modified by heredity and environment. Even though two persons appear as much alike as "two peas in a pod," the fact of individual differences remains. Because family relationships are constantly changing with time and circumstances, even identical twins have different environments.

6. *Activities or functions which depend upon attainment of certain development must wait. Growth cannot be hurried or demanded without serious emotional disturbance.*—For example, toilet training cannot be accomplished for all children at the same age, and for no child at any stated age until the muscles of the bowels and bladder are developed to the point of readiness of control. Again, a child is not ready to read until the muscles of his eyes and the state of his emotions combine to encourage such a venture.

7. *Acceptable "civilized" behavior will come with least resistance from a child whose parents and teachers are*

acquainted with growth information.—Because of this growth information adults will be better able to recognize a child's developmental readiness to accept change. There is no relationship with children entirely free from conflict and irritation. But there can be degrees of resistance. The higher emotional "temperatures" can be reduced when adults recognize a child's readiness for change. "When she likes to do it is when she learns to do it." [2]

Foreknowledge of to-be-expected growth and development is possible. This information should be just as available to parents and other friends of children as is information about formulas and baths. Increasingly, this information *is* available in free and inexpensive bulletins and pamphlets as well as monthly magazines and widely used books (some paperbacks). Public health nurses and community agencies as well as specialists in schools are eager to help families, not only in the interest of the growing child but also for the sake of the total family.

III. THE DEVELOPMENTAL APPROACH

An acknowledgment of these facts of growth toward educational planning is called the developmental approach.

Closely related to this point of view is an idea expressed in the term "developmental tasks." The term means that as there is "inward propulsion" to grow and as one lives in the culture around him, there are certain "tasks," jobs, or work to do which seem peculiarly appropriate to a particular developmental level. This is

[2] Film, *The Terrible Twos, and the Trusting Threes.* (New York: McGraw-Hill Book Company).

characteristic of all human life from infancy to old age. Thinking of infants in terms of progressive growth changes, Dr. Aldrich writes, "Even newborn babies become active, hard-working members of society instead of static bundles wrapped in flannel." [3]

"Children, like adults, have a great deal of . . . unfinished business before them: To learn to ride their "trike"; to do the things of which their parents approve; to understand and get along with adults; to be able to do the things the other children do; to establish their right to make decisions; to have ideas; to become independent; to find out what the world is like—light switches, angle-worms, muddy puddles, icicles, and snow. The list is endless, and the items are not mutually exclusive. Any child can have a considerable hidden agenda of things to be done, worlds to be explored and conquered, people to be understood, and problems to be worked out.

"This 'unfinished business' or 'struggle going on' has more accurately been called 'developmental task.' " [4]

It is the point of view of this book that there are developmental tasks of religious significance. Furthermore, it is held that the kind of religion to which a growing person may be able to respond is conditioned by the early emotional tone to which he is exposed. Long before a child knows the words spoken to him he understands the language of feelings. He absorbs with amazing intuition and accuracy the overtones of the setting of which he is

---

[3] C. Anderson Aldrich and Mary M. Aldrich, *Babies Are Human Beings*. (New York: The Macmillan Company, 1954), p. viii.

[4] Phoebe M. Anderson, *Religious Living with Nursery Children* (Boston: Pilgrim Press, 1956), pp. 12–13.

a part. If he feels love and trustworthiness in human relationships, he brings these meanings to a later conscious religious commitment. If there is miserliness and pessimism in his early emotional experience, he also brings these life experiences into his religious thinking and feeling of later years. Early experiences with the positive human emotions of love and trust may make for more eager commitment to God at a later time. The emotions of hate and mistrust may likewise make later conscious commitment to God more difficult.

IV. SOME QUESTIONS TO RAISE

Because the developmental approach will be acknowledged in this book, some basic questions will be raised about each age level of the Nursery years:

Where does this child-person seem to be in development?

What is his big task now?

How does he propose to perform it?

What problems does his striving bring to himself and others?

How can interested adult persons help him achieve his purposes and enrich his experience?

Is there any aspect of his present development which has significance for religious teaching? What religious experiences (if any) might be expected at this level of development? How do these come about?

What is "teaching and learning" at this level?

What is the ministry of a church to a child at this level?

In chapter 2 these questions are asked about a newborn infant and the growing infant. In chapter 3 the to-be-expected development of a toddler is examined in the light of these questions. Similarly in chapters 4 and 5, these questions continue to be the focal points for the study of a growing Nursery child. Throughout the writing the author seeks to affirm that recognition of growth levels is a helpful tool in the effective sharing of the Christian faith. From beginning to end, it is the purpose of this book to help parents and teachers think about each child for whom they are responsible and then to act in terms of the understanding they receive.

FOR GROUP DISCUSSION

1. Why are you reading this book?
2. Try to think of proverbs, Scripture verses, or folklore which say some things about how children grow. How many of them say essentially the same thing?
3. See the film *Life with Baby.* How does the philosophy described therein relate to the suggestions about growth in this preceding chapter? (Inquire about *Life with Baby* from March of Time Forum Films, 369 Lexington Ave., New York 17, New York. Many state university libraries also rent this film.)
4. Think of some children by name whose growth you have observed rather closely. What similarities in growth development were present? What differences?

CHAPTER 2

2

Newborn!

A MISSIONARY FAMILY who had just returned to the States on furlough was receiving the usual medical checkups. The physician examined the eleven-year-old with careful deliberation. When he had finished, he turned to the mother and inquired gravely, "Now tell me all you can about this child's first year of life."

This sensitive doctor was echoing the growing awareness and concern of many persons who study human growth and development: *The first year of life is highly significant to the entire life span.*

What does happen in the first twelve months after birth? Why is it important? If one is to be a parent for the first time, what can he expect? If one is an experienced parent, is there anything new to be learned? Any unexpected surprises or wonders to anticipate? Any particular areas to cause concern?

I. A BABY OR A TIMETABLE?

Life with Baby (or with older children for that matter) would be simple if babies (and older children) were able to co-operate. If children were all alike, then parents and other interested persons could consult their mutual timetables, know exactly what to expect at certain times, and be prepared to respond in certain appropriate ways. But human babies do not act according to timetables. Though there are many charts and scales which reveal averages

11

as to expected behavior, "Parents . . . would be spared much anxiety if they could bear in mind the difference between an average and a baby." [1]

On the other hand, parents might likewise "be spared anxiety" if somehow they could know that "this is usually so," or "this often happens right about now."

II. A "SEQUENCE" APPROACH

How then shall one look at infant behavior? Shall he follow a book or throw it away? Some of the following ideas might be helpful in making decisions.

Charts and scales do have merit. They are the result of long years of observation and wondering and discovering by many thoughtful people.

However, most scales and norms have been concerned chiefly with the appearances of motor skills which cannot always be trusted to predict other behavior. Only in recent years have the infant's psychological and social functioning come in for major consideration.

How one thinks about norms depends upon his relationship to a baby. First-time grandparents have a little more pride to protect than does the indifferent neighbor next door. Mothers who share the sidewalk and sunshine for carriage strolls are apt to be more anxious about comparisons than are their physicians.

"The trouble with charts," some parents say, "is that my child isn't in the book. He's either behind or ahead according to whether I am worried or feeling smug."

If norms do not tell us accurately about the timing of

---

[1] L. Joseph Stone and Joseph Church, *Childhood and Adolescence, A Psychology of the Growing Persons* (New York: Random House, 1957), p. 52.

new developments in individual cases, they can still serve a worthwhile purpose in giving us the fairly fixed sequence of normal development, regardless of timing. (See chapter 1.) "What to watch for next" is the lead question. What must happen before a baby can walk? before he can talk? How does sociability come about? What is the to-be-expected sequence in religious learning?

Charts and scales can be interesting and fun. But parents need to keep developing a point of view which stresses *sequence* in growth rather than in rate of growth. They need also to think in terms of the individual rather than the norms.

The most meaningful use of books and charts comes in the presence of a problem: "Our up-to-now friendly baby suddenly screams at a stranger—or at one not so strange!" Good references on child care acknowledge that this problem frequently happens around six to ten months.

More important than majoring on minute details (though this can be enjoyable) is an approach which looks for highlights of development. Such an approach raises further some of the questions proposed at the close of chapter 1: What are the concerns, the tasks, of this period? How does the child choose to accomplish them? When is he ready for change? What clues does he offer for readiness to change?

III. THE NEWBORN: HIS TASKS AND PROBLEMS AND ACHIEVEMENTS

Here is the neonate, the newborn. What is he like? Contrary to popular thought and magazine advertising, he is neither pretty nor presentable. He is more realistically described: "On the unattractive side . . . tiny, wet, sticky, often red and wizened creature."[2] He is apparently oblivious to the world around him—or to his own person, for that matter. He mostly eats and sleeps and cries.

But even in his unaware helplessness, the neonate has a task to perform. For some, it is the most difficult work they shall ever face. Each baby must finish getting born: he must adjust to this strange new outside world; he has to learn to breathe; his circulation must change; he must adjust to temperature control. He must take sustenance through his mouth, digest it, and eliminate wastes.

Because such adjustment is not always easy, the new baby often brings problems to himself and to those who care for him. There is discomfort, pain, anxiety, and sleepless nights—and sometimes misgivings and resentment from adults who have done all they know to do. But through the persistent effort and physical stamina of many (including the baby himself), the newborn begins to accomplish his initial tasks and moves on to the further work assigned to his infancy.

As weeks and months follow, Baby achieves some interesting feats. The usual charts might describe to-be-expected highlights by the month in something like this outline:

1st month: Eats, sleeps, and cries
2nd month: Follows moving objects with his eyes but not with his head
3rd month: Gurgles and coos
4th month: Recognizes Mother from others
5th month: Picks up some objects but cannot let go intentionally

---

[2] L. Joseph Stone and Joseph Church, *op. cit.*, pp. 3–4.

6th month: Can let go of an object held in his hand
7th month: Cuts first tooth—though this may come later
8th month: May begin to crawl
9th month: Shows active resentment if desired object is taken away
10th month: Is sociable with adults; plays pat-a-cake
11th month: Recognizes some taboos
12th month: Is on his feet!—pulling up, letting go, cruising, taking some steps perhaps

Such possible highlights are joys to behold. But each of them appears, one must remember, as a link in a chain of readiness.

A baby holds up his head before he learns to sit alone. He learns to sit alone before he crawls. He stands before he walks. There is such a sequence in each phase of his development regardless of the rate at which he progresses. As examples of sequences, here are suggestions about what happens in the baby's development of social awareness, vocalization, sight ability, and hand co-ordination.

A Possible Sequence of Social Awareness

Is fed and talked to
Gurgles and coos
Laughs or chuckles
Recognizes his mother from others
Shows fear of strangers
Drops objects for joy of social exchange when they are recovered
Plays peek-a-boo
Insists on feeding himself
Becomes aware of image in mirror but not curious about source until later

Enjoys and laughs over give-and-take games and shows resentment when something he wants is taken from him

Becomes frustrated and tired if he is left too long in his playpen

Returns affection

Understands a few simple commands

Acknowledges simple taboos

A Possible Sequence of Vocalization

(closely related to hearing and social awareness)

Cries and yells

Enjoys being talked to

Gurgles and coos

Laughs and chuckles; looks to see where voices come from

Babbles (various sounds)

Learns a few words (Da-da) to which adults react enthusiastically

Understands a few simple words that adults address to him

Tries to sing

Enjoys simple songs, rhymes, and jingles

A Possible Sequence of Sight Ability

Looks at without seeing

Follows moving objects with his eyes but not with his head

Follows moving objects with eyes and head until they are out of sight

Looks for source of sound (voice)

Recognizes Mother

A Possible Sequence of Hand Co-ordination

Moves arms aimlessly
Puts hands together
Studies fingers; puts them in mouth
Picks up objects but cannot let go intentionally; gets
 rid of objects by rubbing against side of body
Can let go of objects
Uses both hands in handling things or transfers objects
 from one hand to other
Plays pat-a-cake
Waves bye-bye

IV. Some Implications of Religious Significance

With increasing awe one observes the growth and development of infants. Was there ever a more amazing
example of order and precision? Does a person ever
again in his life achieve this order and precision as
rapidly as in his first year?

Can it possibly be there is yet to be discovered more
meaning about the potential of these months? Persons
who are particularly concerned with spiritual and religious development raise a further question: Are there
implications of religious significance in the growth and
development of the first year of life? If so, how can they
best be acknowledged?

During the first four months of life, a baby has been
"taking hold of the world in ever bigger pieces." He is
eating and sleeping at somewhat-to-be-expected times;
he can move his eyes and his head; he recognizes his
mother; he may laugh and coo. But also during these
months of seemingly automatic growth, there is another

learning. It is not of the nature of "see what he can do," but rather "see what he can feel." Here in the first months of infancy the baby has been developing an emotional response to the world. He smiles because he is satisfied with a relationship. He cries with intent because he is dissatisfied with a relationship. This fact of growing emotional response may have implications of religious significance.

Emotional response begins during the early days and

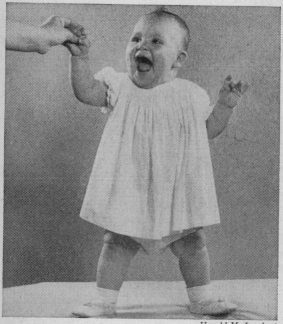

Harold M. Lambert

"Beginnings of a sense of dependability and of a sense of re-latedness with persons may have continuing and enduring effect upon later conscious religious experiences."

weeks of infancy with the fundamental experiences of feeding. At first the infant's concern in this matter is only satisfaction of hunger. But gradually in the process of exchanging emptiness for fullness, a new awareness emerges: the human face—usually that of his mother— becomes a part of the infant's satisfaction from pain and his comfort in well-being. He smiles. As he continues to associate the human face with comfort, an infant also begins to attach meaning to person-experiences. Our language symbolizes this meaning with the words "dependability" and "relationship." These are the beginnings of a sense of dependability.

Such beginnings of a sense of dependability and of a sense of relatedness with persons may have continuing and enduring effect upon later conscious religious experiences. As an infant receives a trustworthy response to his needs, he is learning basic trust, fundamental to all trust relationships, including those called religious. He brings such meaning with him to his later conscious encounter with God. When adults who awaken this basic trust are themselves living daily in a grace-faith relationship with God, surely the child's potential for future religious "faithing" is being nurtured and heightened by this influence.

Likewise, in infancy the kindred emotion of love is awakened through the experiences of being fed. The way in which this basic emotion is nurtured may also have meaning for future religious experience. An infant associates comfort with the people and expressions of love which accompany his physical satisfaction. When the persons who offer this human love are Christians and receive God's perfect love in faith, this life situation may prepare a child for his later conscious acceptance of God's love.

Even as positive experiences with dependability and love may enrich future religious responses, so may negative experiences influence a later religious response. The emotion of hate is learned. When needs are not met, or are met grudgingly or impatiently, the resulting emotions may be attached to persons and words: Father, teacher, church, love, God. Each person's experiences cause him to give particular meaning to these words as he faces God in personal conscious decision and thinks about these words in this relationship. The degree to which a person has learned to mistrust in early childhood may condition his struggle to trust God in personal commitment.

Each first experience increases the possibility of discovering in emotional-sensory-unworded fashion, "This is good, to be trusted, secure." Or, "This is frightening, unsafe, unsure." In large measure, the degree of difference will be in terms of the feeling-emotional-attitudinal responses of the adults who are associated with the child in his experiences.

It is to be added that a Christian parent or teacher or friend to the young child will respond somewhat differently than the parent or friend who does not know God. Responses which may seem alike in two sets of parents will be prompted and guided by different basic commitments.

Christian parents will acknowledge that they are not their own and that they receive life daily through the grace of God. They covenant to nurture their children for the glory of God. In humbleness they seek daily to renew their personal commitment, knowing full well their limitations to love their children perfectly. Their faith is that God will use their limited love to prepare their children for his perfect reconciling love.

Whatever comes to parents from God will also come to their infant in the sure communion and communication of spirit with spirit. Love, trust, a sense of dependability—these come from God to the person who commits himself in faith. Love, trust, a sense of dependability—these likewise come from God to the child through the person who knows God personally and who participates daily and openly in the acknowledgment of his lordship.

V. WHAT MAY a CHURCH DO?

In the light of these understandings, it would seem that the ministry of a church to the infant depends largely on a ministry to his parents.

In the time of the expectancy and acceptance (or rejection) of new life, a ministry is to strengthen the family in love for one another and for God. The church's ministry is to offer the Christian life as inviting and meaningful in the experience of parenthood. In some instances it may be to help expectant parents face the very real problems of concern for themselves, the unborn child, or for others in the family. It is a ministry of encouraging, comforting, or rejoicing.

At the time of the birth of a child, it is the privilege of the church family to acknowledge and receive this child. This may be done as the minister and other sympathetic persons visit in the hospital and in the home. It may be affirmed through the giving of a printed certificate. The event may be recognized through announcements to the church in its gatherings and in the prayers from the pulpit.

Sometimes a church desires to express its concern for the growth of the child through a service of dedication of the parents with their infants. Such an event can be a continuing reminder to parents of their desire and commitment to rear their children "in the admonition of the Lord"; and a reminder of the fellowship of the church in this endeavor.

It is a ministry of a church to protect new parents from too much responsibility too soon in the organized activities of the church life. In addition to the increased expenditure of energy which a newborn usually demands of parents, it is to be expected that one or both parents may be involved in unforeseen emergencies.

In order for parents to handle these and to be responsible for leadership in meetings at specific times may be more than some parents are spiritually and physically able to give. They are more often than not at this time in some need themselves of receiving rather than of giving.

Through encouraging parents, through sharing their joy, and through keeping them aware of fellowship, a church may strengthen the bonds of family love through God's love. The church thereby most appropriately ministers to infants for their present and future religious development.

FOR GROUP DISCUSSION

1. Think of one of your children at home or in the church by name. How much of his first year of life are you able to remember?

2. The sequence for several kinds of response is given in this chapter on pages 15–17. Can you relate these sequences by age and type to different responses of children you teach or live with daily?

3. Put into your own words what you think may be important experiences for an infant in his first year.

CHAPTER 3

3

His Enlarging World

A LOOK AT THE TODDLER CHILD

USUALLY between thirteen months and two years an infant becomes "a toddler." And some, true to a "no time-table" presupposition, toddle as early as nine months. In terms of what he does, the toddler has also been described as: "ambulatory," "self-propelling," "runabout," "bulldozer," and in less sympathetic terms, "terrible!"

Other typical responses of adults to toddlers in a group include:

They won't share.
They push.
They bite.
They hit.
They are all on top of one another and on me.
My shoes are ruined!
I can't get them to sit down.
When one starts crying they all start.

A toddler is trying many new abilities. He is finding out how to talk and how to walk. He is gropingly discovering the power he has over himself and over other people.

His curiosity, his need to explore, and his insistence upon asserting himself are bound to bring problems to the persons who are responsible for him. Care of him requires energy and endurance, insight and courage.

The toddler period is one of discovering competence, of stepping out of parents' arms and then back into them.

It can be a time of wholesome beginnings in the process of separation, in the ever-present struggle of independ-ence-dependence.

Desirable outcomes can be more logically hoped for when there is acknowledgment of the particular growth needs of toddlerhood and a careful planning for meeting them positively and hopefully.

What is a toddler really like? What is his big, com-pelling task? How does he choose to accomplish it? What problems does striving bring to himself and to others? Is there anything of particular religious significance to this period? What is the ministry of the church to a per-son of this age?

I. A "TASK" FOR THE TODDLER

Perhaps an interested person can grope his way vaguely through the spontaneous appraisals given above and find in them indications of a toddler person's task. Can it be that he is trying out new abilities—locomotion, languages, emotional expressions? Could he be trying to find out—"learning" in some primitive fashion?

If such a possibility is true, throughout all of this new awareness of discovering and trying out what he himself can do, there is another obvious quality: a toddler ap-parently is likewise bound by the very nature of his growth process to assert himself—to tell the world in some way that he has a new competence to do things for himself. He feels his power; he has a heady sense of in-dependence; he will express it even before opposition.

Whereas in early infancy the task of a child seems to be to learn to trust his environment, the enlarging task of toddlerhood is apparently to learn to trust one's self. It

Bob Churchwell

"The enlarging task of toddlerhood is apparently to learn to trust one's self."

is often said of a child at this stage in development that he is seeking autonomy.

A closer look at a toddler reveals some details in answer to questions: What is his task? How does he seek to accomplish it? What problems does his striving bring?

II. MOTOR CONTROL

The toddler's new skill of locomotion is prominent. He is "vertical" instead of "horizontal." He practices and practices running around and around; he darts and dashes and flings and steps on, not over, objects. When stairs are available he climbs them endlessly, and takes great glee in achievement. Such treatment is also given to obstacles like bumps in the ground. His locomotive power puts him in fine position for exploring so that, true to generations of toddlers, he is "into everything."

The tired adult seldom finds much that is good about a toddler's self-propulsion. However, with some rest for himself and a fond look at his charge (who is sleeping temporarily), he reconsiders: What if this child were not active at this point in his development? What positive things for good are happening because he is exploring? How can I reduce some of the negative factors? One has only to think of the man-hours spent in scientific inquiry to acknowledge that exploration, activity, and inquisitiveness are all assets to learning.

For a toddler, the new worlds to conquer are right outside the once-confining bars of his crib or playpen. The light cord, the dresser drawers, the clothes closet, the bric-a-brac on low tables—all of these beckon to a healthy, alert, eager-to-learn toddler. His method is necessarily elementary and primitive. He touches, he pulls, he tastes, he drips, he smears, he pushes both things and people.

But when he is given sympathy and limited planned surroundings, a toddler learns extensively from his exploring and manipulation:

1. *He senses joy and companionship in learning.* —When busy adults join in his glee over discovery, approval is given to the practice of inquiry. Curiosity is kept alive to work in ever-enlarging and difficult areas.

2. *Through exploration speech is encouraged, vocabulary is extended, and chances for reading success are promoted.*—For example: "Hard," "soft," "sweet," "sour," "sticky," and "book," are learned by sense and sound.

3. *In guided exploration, a toddler has beginning experiences with property rights and limitations.*—He learns through consistent practice. "Mommy's book," "Daddy's book," "Gail's book."

4. *A toddler's co-ordination is encouraged through exploration.*—Allowed to pick up some objects or climb (under supervision), he is using, strengthening, and refining muscles appropriate to his maturation level.

5. *His sense of self-awareness is furthered when a toddler is allowed to be curious.*—In early infancy, the baby was unable to distinguish himself from the world of people and things; only gradually does he gather a sense of "I amness," of apartness and separation. Each time he finds something not of himself this sense of separateness is accentuated.

Despite one's acknowledgment of a learning possibility in the exploratory nature of toddlerhood and of the joys a toddler brings, the honest adult has some negative feelings. Anyone who has been responsible for an exploring toddler can answer in short order and in dramatic terms what problems the experience brings to adults. If the day has been a typical one, the person who is questioned will probably make a gesture of collapse, pull his hair and cry aloud: "I give up! You take him!"

At no other stage do children seem to require of adults such constant physical supervision, such tremendous expenditure of energy. The agility and curiosity of the runabout send him off in many directions; he doesn't come when called; adults must go to him. If the child is allowed any freedom, then an adult must follow him, not only to protect the toddler, but also to protect others and things from the toddler. Actual physical weariness is a very real problem for persons who are responsible for toddlers.

There is an accompanying emotional strain of the attitudes of other people. What will they think? What about the times I go to other homes or to a store or to church with this exploring child?

The following suggestions may give some sense of direction to parents and teachers who recognize both the opportunity and the problems of being responsible for an ever-inquisitive toddler.

1. *Expect that the presence of a toddler (or toddlers) will demand physical exertion and emotional expenditure.*—Adjust schedules and activities and supervision accordingly. In the home, arrange for some time to renew physical energy. In group situations, plan for enough people to share the strain of constant, alert supervision.

2. *Curtail as many demands outside the home as the basic personality will allow.*—All parents need some outlets away from home. However, when a toddler is in the home, outside interests may need to be limited. When the parents need to be away, they should look for a helping person whose approach can be somewhat like their own.

3. *Set whatever limits are necessary and be consistent in acknowledging these.*—The child's safety and the parents' own well-being require some minimum prohibitions. How many limitations there are and the way in

which they are enforced is of importance. Fire and water are examples of areas where toddlers cannot safely explore. Other activities which threaten the social comfort of many persons may demand that a toddler's freedom be limited temporarily.

4. *Offer alternatives to necessary limitations.*—Parents want personal books to read again, but old magazines may be hauled around and torn as a child desires. Likewise, parents probably can't allow children to jump from beds and chairs or sofas, but they can make some appropriate jumping places elsewhere.

5. *Put treasured or dangerous items out of reach.*—A toddler simply cannot be responsible for deciding what is explorable. Should he be tempted with the sight of beckoning fragile items which he cannot touch? Should he be punished for wanting to touch them? Fire and electricity do involve life and death and the child should learn early to approach them with caution. Perhaps "barking" and hand slapping are in order as appropriate association with such dangers. Such measures seem inappropriate when the objects of explorations are beauty and sound and movement.

6. *Give some thought to the frequency with which a toddler is taken away from the planned environment of his home.*—Other settings are not always equipped to receive him happily. A parent does not change his social and vocational pattern completely because he has a toddler. However, if he desires the maximum security for his toddler and the minimum of frustration for himself, he must make some adjustments to his original carefree living.

III. LANGUAGE GROWTH

Another new competence which is coming to a toddler is a growing ability with word language. Just as locomotion gives him a heady sense of power, so also does his increasing ability with words.

Language is not totally new to a toddler. As has been suggested, the infant begins to participate in human communication from the day of his birth. He learns to distinguish and sort out meaning as it is revealed in voice tone, facial expression, and actions which accompany these. Thus does love, joy, or impatience become known to him. This is language, the language of understanding.

In toddlerhood the additional language of the spoken word begins to flower. At this time words are attached to relationship and action: "kiss," "eat," "bye-bye." Within these labels or names (nouns) and action words (verbs) he has learned, a toddler discovers means for communicating requests or demands such as "eat!" There follows the expressive mixture of gibberish and real words before a toddler settles down to words without jargon.

One-word utterances are complete statements for the child: "Broke" (the bottle is); "Go" (in the car or out-of-doors). These one-word sentences are gradually replaced by two-word and three-word phrases and finally by complete sentences.

Despite his increasing vocabulary, a toddler's favorite word seems to be no. This is quite in character with his new-found sense of power; when viewed as such it can be dealt with by adults without resentment. On the other hand, if the inevitable presence of no becomes an issue between parents and child, resulting in a clash of wills, negativism may be encouraged rather than assimilated.

Since even the best-intentioned adult is sometimes tricked by the complexities of toddlerhood, some reminders of positive approaches to real problems which grow out of language difficulties may be helpful.

1. *Remember that spoken language is only a beginning.*—Perhaps the greatest problems which adults have in regard to toddler speech is in acknowledging how really inadequate this new ability is in contrast to the degree which adults have achieved and want for their child.

2. *Enforce words with action.*—Communication with toddlers must still depend largely upon the total language relationship—the facial expression, the tone of voice, the grasp of the hand, the showing how. Particularly is this true in giving a toddler initial experience with some usual social demand. "Time to go," accompanied by an outstretched hand and moving toward the door (or picking the child up) will achieve more response than repeatedly calling, "Come on." The first example shows what the words mean. Likewise, "Put away toys," can be learned with less frustration if the adult accompanies words with cleaning the room.

3. *Expect to repeat requests.*—Children do not usually respond to one telling. They cannot easily cut off one exploration in favor of a less interesting activity. Toddlers need to be reminded (without nagging or irritation) of the problem at hand.

4. *Go to the child.*—Communication with a toddler must take place in a close-up position. Calling out from

an adjoining room—or even across the room—has little value and leads to habits of inattention.

5. *Formulate a worthy philosophy about obedience.*—What is obedience for? When should it be expected? Is submission always a quality to be commended? Perhaps the most important attitude for Christians is that one which concerns relationship. Is this child my servant or my co-laborer? My possession or my brother? A person or a thing? In the light of these reflections, am I justified in making as many demands as I do? Are my expectations within the child's ability to achieve? If so, are they for his well-being or mostly for my own convenience? How much of what I command is born out of thought? How much out of habit?

6. *Distinguish between lack of understanding and "disobedience."*—Somehow when toddlers begin to use and understand a few words and requests, impatient adults expect them to reason through a barrage of verbal commands. When a child hesitates in such instances or acts in an opposite manner, he may be doing so because he is not capable of following so many words.

7. *When making a suggestion or giving directions, use the positive approach.*—Saying "Put shoes here" (indicate a spot), rather than "don't put your shoes on the sofa," will tell the child what *to* do; so will "Pat Jimmy gently," (showing how) instead of "don't squeeze Jimmy." When children receive negative directions, they still do not know what to do. A positive direction points the way. Even for adults, positive directions are much easier to follow than negative ones (observe doctors, technicians, or teachers of detailed skills).

8. *Avoid reasoning with toddlers.*—There will be time a-plenty for talking it out and for explanation. While vocabulary is limited, a much more sensible approach is to do what needs to be done (like putting on clothes) despite verbal protest. In time of real emotional distress which cannot be resolved (Daddy's going to work), diversion and distraction are more appropriate than explanation. Toddlers do not yet have the mental ability to reason much. Premature attempts to encourage them to do so result in an excitable child.

9. *Give few choices and then only when you expect to abide by the child's decision.*—Making a choice is frustrating to a toddler. He wants both things. As concerns no or yes, toddlers will say no anytime a choice is offered in a direct question. Unless an adult can accept a no, then he should be careful about offering choices. Instead of asking, "Don't you want to go now?" he can say, "Time to go now."

10. *Wait until later for the verbal expression of "manners."*—Toddlers cannot be held responsible for thank you and please and I'm sorry although they can often say the words. Adults can say these words for the children when the occasion arises. Here again, if adults express the proper concern for generous or regrettable acts, the toddlers who are in their presence are learning words for the actions. Their often-surprising, spontaneous thank you's are delightful rewards for waiting.

11. *Encourage speech accuracy through consistent adult example rather than through constant correction.* —Nothing is more discouraging to a new-found achievement than constant faultfinding. Toddlers are just be-

ginning to hear and repeat. If they hear the appropriate word or phrase used constantly and naturally, they will learn to use the words.

12. *Expect a toddler to use the speech patterns of those with whom he is most closely associated.*—If these persons are his parents, a toddler will talk like them. If most of his waking hours are with another person—a maid, a neighbor, or a grandparent, he will take on their patterns and habits of speech. This includes the total language—vocabulary, accent, favorite expressions, and tonal quality.

13. *Let the developing ability of speech be used for communication and not for performance.*—The child who is urged to talk for the enjoyment of adults will soon lose his original joy in language and take refuge in shy self-conscious withdrawal. The child whose strugglings are accepted with respect continues to gain confidence and skill.

IV. SOCIAL RESPONSE

A third area in which a toddler particularly distinguishes himself is in his social awareness (or his lack of it). He treats people in much the same way that he responds to things. He pokes and pushes, shoves and throws, and often bites and hits. He has little sense of "you" and "others," but he is quite able and familiar with "me" and "mine." In larger social settings under pressure, he may act the same as he does in the smaller family setting—refusing, protesting, demanding, and opposing.

Suggestions have been given previously in this chapter about limiting visits outside the familiar setting of home. Persons who are responsible for a toddler's early social experience may find further help from the following suggestions:

1. Introduce the child gradually to experiences away from home.

2. Let the experience be in the company of a parent or another adult the child knows well.

3. Select group situations which will allow a toddler to be his active, normal self.

4. Look for group situations where there are few people.

5. Arrange for the experiences to be brief and frequent rather than long and occasional.

V. A Critical Issue

The area of behavior most likely to involve conflict between parent and child is toilet training. Inexperienced parents (themselves the victims of insistence, perhaps) take pride in a "trained" child. Eager to be free from daily laundry, they exchange physical drudgery for emotional exhaustion.

A toddler, at the time of his parent's persistence, may not be ready physically to control bowel and bladder. In addition, his increasing self-awareness makes him resistant and negative. The ability for language is not yet sufficient for intelligent conversation about the matter. Thus, unless caution is exercised by the adult, a clash of wills may result from efforts at too-early toilet training.

Fortunately, because sympathetic pediatricians and helpful literature are increasingly available to families, fewer children suffer the effects of rigidity in too-early toilet training than previously. However, enough problems related to this matter do appear to make a reference to this area quite necessary and appropriate. Parents of toddlers should be encouraged to re-examine their philosophy of toilet training.

VI. IMPLICATIONS OF RELIGIOUS SIGNIFICANCE

Is there any factor present in the picture of the developing toddler-child which might be of religious significance? If so, how may this fact be acknowledged by adults to the end that its presence may be nurtured and its potential protected for future development?

The young infant's need is for security. To feel dependability and trust in and from those who care for him is perhaps the greatest potential he may have for future positive religious experiencing. But the enlarging task of toddlerhood is apparently to learn to trust himself. To begin to know in a small sense that one IS—separate and apart from others; to prove that one *is* by the things one can do; to confirm further that one *is* by resisting that which others would impose—this is the growing self-awareness and self-assertiveness of toddlerhood.

The response of adults to this self-assertion in a toddler may be a factor which will condition a later faith commitment to God. If there is patient, firm, sympathetic guidance, this will be assimilated for good in continuing religious interpretation. If there is "breaking the will," many other potential qualities for positive commitment will also be broken. One must be before he can care; one must own before he can give; one must possess before he can share. Made in the image of God and for God, man yet has freedom to give or withhold his very self— not only from all other humans but also from God.

It would seem that adults who are concerned for the

religious development of toddlers must welcome evidences of selfhood, acknowledge the trials of its initial assertiveness, and give sympathetic guidance to channeling it to creative humble functioning.

What are some ways in which an adult may give guidance so that the positive qualities in self-awareness may be nurtured for future religious commitment? Perhaps the following ideas may be starting points:

1. Offer many occasions for exploring, trying out, succeeding.

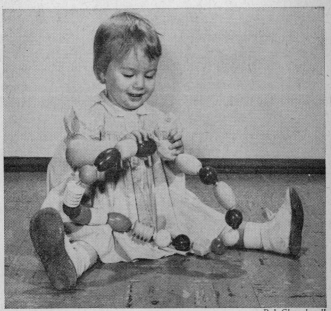

Bob Churchwell

"The appropriate church setting for toddlers is the atmosphere of home: someone to trust, a few people, some things to explore, freedom to move around, companionable rejoicing in a toddler's growing competence."

2. Make boundaries or limitations when a toddler would hurt himself or others.

3. Call the child's name with firmness and joy, thus increasing the sense of identity.

4. Be glad with a toddler in his accomplishments, thus strengthening his feelings of value and worth.

5. Designate some things as a toddler's possessions, but name others as "Daddy's," "Mommy's," or "Brother's" to encourage awareness of separateness.

Give something of one's own to a child in a deliberate joyous sharing. Such an experience should help a toddler to associate joy and love and trust with the experience of giving-receiving.

VII. What May a Church Do?

When one looks carefully at both the potentials and the limitations of a toddler-person, he is inclined to decide that the most appropriate ministry of a church to a toddler is a ministry to his parents.—Even a child's consistent attendance in the organized settings at the church is less important than the home atmosphere. Through the visits and prayers and thoughtful concern of both minister and fellow members, through receiving counseling, and through public worship, the home may be strengthened in love and faith and fellowship. Through these ministries to his home a toddler may grow in awareness of God and man.

FOR GROUP DISCUSSION

1. Recall the three areas of experience mentioned in this chapter that distinguishes a toddler.
2. Hear a panel of parents of toddler children. The subject might be: "My Toddler: What Is He Like?; How Do I Feel About Him?" Note if different sets of parents make similar responses.

Note also how frequently or infrequently the observations and suggestions in this chapter may be mentioned.

3. The writer states on page 40: "When one looks carefully at both the potentials and limitations . . . he is inclined to decide that . . . the most appropriate ministry of the church to the child is to his parents." What do you think are "potentials and limitations"?

CHAPTER 4

4

More and More

WHO IS AN INFANT? How long is one a toddler? What is two-year-oldness? The indefinability of terms for age groups is never more difficult than during the periods preceding the third birthday. Though months pile up chronologically, human growth and development keeps its own sure calendar. Such time is measured not by days but by sequence and individual rate and the circumstances of which a child is a part.

An infant isn't suddenly a toddler; his months of lying and waving and kicking and pulling have brought him to the place where he continues to move in a different fashion toward further achievement. A two-year-old doesn't cease to "toddle" simply because he has had a birthday. Gradually, slowly, surely, transitions come and go—none of them independent of the past, each of them necessary for the future.

With this reaffirmation of the importance of individual growth sequences, one then looks at many, many children. How much is Susan, age two years and three months, like Janis, age two years and three months? How different are these two? One asks: Does there seem to be among many children in the same narrow age span some mutuality of seeking, of responding, of growing? Are there likewise noticeable differences?

43

I. Two-Year-Olds Are Different

As a challenge to observation, here are some word pictures of children between their second and third birthdays. These descriptions were written by parents with the minimum of guidance: Make a picture of your child as he appears to you. Acknowledge what seems to you to be important to him. Say, if you like, where you have had problems with yourself or with him because of his style of behaving.

The casual reader may just enjoy the descriptions of Jim and David and Pam. Parents and teachers of two-year-olds may exclaim at some point, "Just like mine!" Still others may observe, "But that isn't all!"

About Jim

My two-and-a-half-year-old son amazes me constantly these days with some new facet of his personality. It is such fun to watch him develop as a real little person, and that's what I've begun to see in recent months!

One thing that I've noticed especially is a marked—really exaggerated—sort of independence that pops up at the most unexpected times. For example, he simply must take off his own socks. Sometimes I forget this in undressing him; and, of course, he is insulted. Thus I have to put the socks back on so he can remove them himself! He is equally adamant about closing the car door. On many occasions we've had to reopen the door so that he could close it.

This independence exhibits itself in toilet training. He is convinced that his system of wetting his pants is by far the most satisfactory, and he seems determined to stick to this plan. He doesn't have to interrupt his play! Despite all this big-boy independence, however, there are moments, especially at bedtime, when he is a very little fellow who wants his mama.

In his play it seems important to him to accomplish results that he can immediately see. Thus toys with moving parts are appealing. He also enjoys the simple process of moving sand or blocks from one place to another. He seems satisfied when he has completed the moving job— whatever it happens to be. He tends to dawdle quite a bit in his eating, and it is futile to try to rush him. I find that if I allow him plenty of time, and leave him alone while he's eating, he tends to do better.

I've been interested in his ability to associate situations and ideas. Recently we ate lunch in a restaurant and as we were preparing to leave he remarked, "Come back to see us!" Of course, he had heard this many times in the past from waitresses and cashiers. Another instance that I recall occurred one evening when a member of the family was sick in bed with a cold. Jim said to her, "It'll be all right. Don't worry!" I am confident that I've spoken these exact words to him at times when he's been sick or has skinned a knee or elbow.

It seems to me that tact is very important in dealing with a child of this age. In every possible instance I try to lead him gently (even subtly) from one activity to the other. It's the old idea of convincing him that what he's doing is really his idea, not mine! As a first-time mother, however, in the process of learning the ropes, I can truly say that this two-year-old age is the most fascinating yet! Perhaps I'll say the same of the next stage, too, after he reaches it!

About David

David is two-and-a-half years old, stockily built, and very active. He has a brother about two years older than he, and because of this he often talks and acts older than his age. In fact, he is the youngest of the many children in his neighborhood, but in play he feels himself equal to them. Often he attempts to bully the older children by threatening them with sticks or rocks in an attempt to show his equality. He seldom actually strikes another child unless provoked but seems to enjoy seeing others run from his threats.

For all his "maturity," however, David still shows qualities of the young child that he is. He is very attached to his home and parents, and does not yet feel secure enough to stray far away for very long periods. At times when the other children choose to play in areas somewhat distant from his home, David usually remains in his own yard or quickly returns to it to play by himself. He can be just as content in solitary play as in his play with other children. He also still enjoys playing games with his parents and often "hides" from them in the house so that he will have to be hunted in an elementary type of "hide-and-seek" game.

David has a very active imagination. At times he may pretend he is a puppy dog while at other times he may be a gorilla or a "monster." Although his older brother is beginning to make the distinction between reality and fantasy, David has not yet reached this stage of development. For him, products of imagination are as real as physical objects.

David's temperament is still highly emotional. While

at times he may "bargain" for a toy or desired object which another child has, he will resort to forceful tactics very quickly if his diplomatic attempt is thwarted. He has not yet developed the ability to pursue logically an answer to the problems and crises which arise in his life, but acts instead on the impulse of emotion. He is still very self-centered and insists on things going his way. This is especially true when he is cross or irritable. These emotional outbursts and complete lack of an ability to reason sometimes cause annoying frustration for his parents.

David has been greatly influenced by the actions and attitudes of his older brother as well as those of neighborhood playmates. But a marked difference can be seen between him and the older children in various areas of his life. In general, he is a "typical" two-year-old who manifests some characteristics which seem to be beyond his expected level of development.

About Pam

Both of us (parents) can readily agree that this year in Pam's life has been a most enjoyable one. During the year, she has not grown so much physically, but we have seen a rapid development socially and emotionally. She has become a real person who thinks and acts quite independently. Her personality really influences all phases of our lives.

Pam is a very active child. She is seldom if ever still. She seems to have an endless supply of energy. Her day begins around 7:30 or 8:00 A.M. By 11:00 A.M. she is beginning to be tired. After she eats lunch, she is ready for a nap which usually lasts about two hours. Then she wakes up to spend the afternoon at play. Bedtime comes at 7:30 each night.

Pam enjoys her bath before going to bed; she prefers to bathe herself. If I forget, she reminds me of such things as taking vitamins, brushing teeth, or saying prayers before going to bed. We must follow the same "ritual" each night. First, a hug and kiss for Mommy and Daddy, then a glass of water, a cooky, and her cover. She wants two blankets, no matter what the temperature, always the *same* two blankets. Before going to sleep, Pam must have her pillow and a stuffed kitten which she has had since she was a few months old. She never seems to need these until it is time to sleep. The kitty is now very dirty and has lost most of its stuffing. If we ask Pam what she will do when the kitty falls to pieces, she always replies, "I will cry and cry." Some nights sleep comes instantly. Then, again, she may sing and chatter for some time before she falls asleep.

There are many days when Pam finds things to amuse herself for hours without help from anyone. Then there are times when she can't seem to think of anything to do and needs helpful suggestions and guidance. She enjoys playing out-of-doors. While inside, she plays with her toys. Usually this means getting them all out and leaving them. At our insistence, she will pick them up again, but this is not an enjoyable task for her.

She has, in the past few months, begun to watch television for short periods of time. Programs that interest her are cartoons or shows that have children in them. She had never before shown any interest in television.

She enjoys games such as "London Bridge" and "Ring Around the Roses." She likes to put simple puzzles together and to look at books and magazines. We have read storybooks to her so often that she can tell them back to us. She likes to draw with pencil or crayon. From her experience in nursery school, I'm sure she also likes to paint with tempera paints, but I haven't been brave enough yet to try this at home.

Pam likes to sing. She knows many songs, but will sometimes sing by just making all sorts of sounds with no words or meaning. She usually has a book in her hand. It may be a magazine or her daddy's Greek book and it is sometimes upside down, but it is her songbook.

In recent months, we have noticed that she is reaching the pretend stage. When she sings, she pretends she is in the church choir. We sometimes sing in her "choir" while she plays her piano. She pretends she is a doctor or nurse or a mother. When I wash her hair, she pretends she is at the beauty shop and I am the beauty operator. She puts on her high heels and hat and pretends that she goes to town or to the grocery store.

Pam likes to imitate whatever we are doing. If I'm sweeping or washing dishes, she wants to do these things. If I'm ironing, she has to have her iron and ironing board. Recently, I've heard her "preaching" like her daddy. Pam has always enjoyed going to church. She usually stays in a Nursery room. But lately she has asked if she could go to church like Mommy and Daddy. I have taken her several times and she sat very quietly throughout the services.

We are grateful for the experiences Pam had in nursery school this year. Being with children has helped her in many ways. She enjoys playing with others. They may sometimes have disagreements, but disagreements are always quickly forgotten. Pam can be the liveliest member in the group but when she begins to get tired, it seems that nothing goes right for her. Being very young when she first entered the group experience at nursery school, she had her share of frustrations, but we feel that the months were very worthwhile in preparing her to live with others. Pam makes friends easily and constantly keeps a conversation going. Her little smile, bright twinkling eyes, and bubbling enthusiasm are present at almost any time.

We have shown concern over Pam's inability to defend herself in certain group situations. For example, if a child hits or abuses her in some way, she will begin to cry rather than straighten things out for herself. We don't want to teach her to fight, but we would like to see her defend herself in situations such as this. We hope that as she grows older she will learn to cope better with such problems.

We began Pam's toilet training when she was eighteen months old. We experienced little difficulty and were pleased with her rapid progress. Now on rare occasions she may wet the bed at night, but this happens very infrequently. She no longer has to be reminded, but goes to the bathroom by herself without assistance. She cannot completely dress herself yet. She can put on her pants, socks, and shoes, though she doesn't tie or buckle the shoes.

Pam usually eats well and doesn't make quite as much of a mess as she has in the past. She now likes to eat at the table with us rather than in the high chair. We often eat meals in the homes of different people. It is not unusual to have glasses overturned or for Pam to tell our hostess quite frankly that she doesn't like strawberries or whatever the hostess has prepared for dessert. These situations could be embarrassing, but we just don't let them upset us. Pam is either being truthful or has had an accident which she could not prevent. Most people are very understanding.

Pam is very fond of her grandparents who live quite a distance away. Although she does not get to see them often, she talks about them constantly and always wants to go to visit them. Last November, she told her grandmother that she had a baby brother. She showed her a picture of him which was really a baby picture of herself. Since then, Pam has talked quite frequently about a baby brother, or sometimes, a sister. We don't know what gave her the idea, but she is still talking about it. She tells everyone that the baby is in the hospital in Macon, Georgia, where she was born. When we are shopping, she wants to buy bottles or beds or whatever she sees that a baby could use. She loves for us to tell her about the time when she was a tiny baby. When we show her some pictures of her baby days, she gets so excited she jumps up and down.

Questions, questions! Do we ever stop answering questions? Pam must know why to everything that's done. We find it difficult already to answer some of her questions. None of them can be ignored. She must have some kind of answer.

Next month Pam will be three years old. We will be looking forward to another year filled with questions. I'm sure it will hold joys as well as frustrations for Pam. We will learn as she learns new things. There are so many things we want to remember about Pam in these years.

It is nice for us to stop and write some of them down.

II. Two-Year-Olds Are Alike

When one reads and rereads these vignettes and recalls the "between two- and three-year-olds," he is inclined to reaffirm the fact stated earlier in this book: *Perhaps the greatest likeness of any human being to all other humans is that each is somehow different, modified by heredity and environment.* But one also observes that while children are different they often respond in quite a similar fashion. Two-year-olds seem to have these following characteristics in common—in varying degrees of intensity.

Bob Churchwell

"Two's are energy powered, activity motivated, and emotionally charged."

They have a strong sense of independence, but there are times when there is likewise a need to be dependent upon parents or other trustworthy adults. This is especially true when children are fatigued.

They are energy powered, activity motivated, and emotionally charged. They are curious about the world around them. They ask the inevitable questions:
Where, what, why, and gradually who and how.

They imitate adults.

Such characteristics are much like those observed in toddlers. Other responses, quite naturally, begin to be like those most readily associated with three-year-oldness: making tries at playing together (although happiness is short-lived); beginning to enter dramatic play; acting out the life around them.

III. What May a Church Offer Two-Year-Olds?

The daily experiences of the two-year-old are of significance to his religious awareness in later years. The degree and quality of attention paid to him, the relationships of others in his household, the tempo at which life is lived, the commitments and concerns of the persons around him, the kind of words and the manner in which they are voiced—the overtones in these areas of living will be absorbed and assimilated by the young child. They will condition all of his later conscious striving, including those called religious. Thus the home is the major factor in any consideration of religious values, and the church offers its best ministry to the two-year-old when it ministers to his parents and other older members of the family.

Activities in the organized settings at the church for two-year-olds will have meaning as they are also planned in terms of the child's absorbing from the relationships to which he is exposed. Thus the question to raise is not, What can I say or tell? but rather, What can I be? And in the light of growth facts, the accompanying question is, What can I do with and for this child to add to his sense of security, to strengthen his joy in personhood, and to afford happy anticipation about coming here?

Some two's continue to need much the same basic environment in the church setting as do toddlers. Other two's can do well in the setting planned for early three-year-olds. The point is that each child should be recognized as an individual.

The planning for a separate group of two's in a church should acknowledge the needs for:

A small enrolment per room
Limited hours of meeting
Consistent, reliable leadership worthy of imitation
Enough leadership to give individual attention to children
Space for activity
Objects and materials to stimulate attention and satisfy needs

In such a setting children can be two-year-olds going about the business of learning as two-year-olds: looking, wondering, experimenting, asking, trying, discovering, practicing, failing, achieving, relating, repeating, delighting. In response to two-year-olds and their ways of learning, teachers teach when they offer, provide, encourage, sympathize, comfort, allow, interpret, delight, and enjoy. Together, adult and child experience the

J. Carey Wood

"Two-year-olds should be going about the business of learning as two-year-olds: looking, wondering, experimenting, asking, trying, discovering."

meaning in the words, "I was glad when they said unto me, Let us go into the house of the Lord."

FOR GROUP DISCUSSION

1. Let each class member think of a two-year-old he knows well. The child may be his own, one he teaches, or a good friend. Have each person write a description of this child.
2. When some of these descriptions are shared in the class, let other class members indicate a similar response of two-year-olds they may have noted.
3. See the film, *The Terrible Twos, and the Trusting Threes*. Review the ways of two-year-olds as described in it; check these against those which class members have observed in children.

CHAPTER 5

5

Happy Sunday?

YOUNG CHILDREN have their most meaningful religious learning in the home. An organized setting at church cannot replace this experience. Sometimes, however, parents of young children cannot attend public worship themselves unless they bring their children. When this is true, persons who are interested in the Christian growth of families must think about a ministry to the infant and toddler at the church.

I. Two Questions

1. If parents must have young children with them in meetings, will they be able to give themselves to study and worship, or will they simply be in attendance?

2. If provisions are made for children, will these be only an arrangement for the convenience of parents, or might they also offer experience of religious significance to the young child? If the latter is a possibility, what might this experience be and what circumstances might nurture it?

Most people can think immediately of the natural barriers which confront parents and others when they think of bringing infants to church. The very physical helplessness of infants demands some obvious preparation. The equally demanding growth needs of toddlers may not be so clearly discerned by the unpracticed observer's eye.

II. A REMINDER ABOUT TODDLERS

Any planning for toddlers at church demands a re-thinking of toddler's social ability—or his lack of it. (See chapter 3.) Though the growing child is increasingly aware of people and delights in companionship, his stage of development does not allow him to be a very responsible person in a group of people. He is not ready to sit or converse; he cannot reason or reflect. Lacking in these abilities by the very nature of his development, he can be neither thoughtful nor kind and considerate of other people. Instead he is apt to treat other toddlers in much the same manner that he "tries out" objects—pushing, pulling, and biting.

With these normal growth barriers to sociability, a toddler is both exhausted and exhausting if he is exposed to groups for extended periods of time. This is true whether he is with a group at home or at church.

III. APPROPRIATE ENVIRONMENTS FOR BABIES AND TODDLERS

In the book *Improving Nursery Departments* by Dillard, there are detailed suggestions for setting up Nursery departments in a church. In the pages which follow, some questions about general provisions (in relation to growth needs previously discussed) may serve as guides to evaluation. For ease in recall, these suggestions might be thought of as six essential requirements which begin with the letter S.

1. *Separateness.*—Has every effort been made to separate infants and toddlers from one another and from other children?

2. *Safety.*—Are there maximum precautions against disease, fire, falls, cuts, burns, or intrusion from strangers? Are there easy exits in event of emergency? Is the floor snagproof? Is there some policy about attendance of children or adults who may be ill? Is there some means of sterilizing equipment? Is there soap-and-water cleanliness?

3. *Space.*—In infant settings are the beds separated by at least three feet? In toddler settings is there room for children to be themselves—to move about, to explore, to be protected from the primitive social overtures of other children? Is the number of children in each room limited to allow for emotional calm?

4. *Supplies.*—What materials and facilities are there to provide maximum learning conditions? Is there access to water, soap, towels, clothes, first-aid supplies? Are there materials (toys, things, picture books) to encourage exploration and foster gladness in achievement? Who will be responsible for the purchase and maintenance of facilities and materials?

5. *Storage.*—Are there facilities which provide for maximum sanitation, care, and immediate availability? Where will the personal belongings (coats, hats, diaper bags) of both children and adults be placed? Is there some policy of the church about the use of this storage space?

6. *Someone.*—Who will be *Security* in this place away from the assurance of parents' arms? How many persons must be present with this group to assure maximum care for both physical and emotional needs? What qualities of attitude must these persons have? What skills? What emotional tolerance? What physical abilities?

These requirements are not easily met. Many parents and other friends of children must give thought, energy, and money to solving the problems involved in an appropriate environment.

IV. WHAT CAN BABIES AND TODDLERS LEARN AT CHURCH?

A terse reply which reveals the basic truth is: They can learn to want to come to this place or they can learn to dislike coming to this place. Put in terms which already have appeared in this book, they can learn to "trust" or "distrust" this place and the persons and ideas associated with it.

If they are comfortable (dry, fed, and noticed), if they are free, if they are secure, they will find trust. Nothing more important than this experience of finding trustworthiness can happen to young children in church settings. From this basic response will stem all other ideas of religious significance which the person associates with this place.

Thus, a worthy purpose for having prepared for infants and toddlers in the organized life of the church should include: to provide an atmosphere in which the young child may have additional extended experiences with trust and well-being and attach importance to the church—its people and message.

V. WHAT CAN BABIES AND TODDLERS DO AT CHURCH?

This question must be answered by those who plan for infants, toddlers, and two's at church. The most direct and appropriate answer is that one hopes they can do what they do in an average home. For the infant this means to sleep, to eat, to be bubbled, to be diapered, to be loved. Sometimes for some children it means to be played with. For any infant it means being treated in a way peculiar to himself.

The appropriate church setting for toddlers is the atmosphere of home: Someone to trust, a few people, some things to explore, freedom to be able to move around, companionable rejoicing in a toddler's growing competence.

"Home" has pots and pans and wastebaskets and dresser drawers, plus many commercial things which loving hearts bestow. Outside there is dirt and grass and water and green plants.

A church which purposes to extend the trust experience must plan for a similar environment. Many of the same familiar play materials of the home can be used in the church for toddlers. In addition, large permanent-type play equipment which is too bulky for small homes may be added to give encouragement and enjoyment in self-competence.

A list of possible activities for toddlers and two's in an appropriate church setting includes the following activities:

1. Rocking a doll
2. Playing with dishes
3. Playlike talking on telephone
4. Opening, shutting, carrying objects
5. Filling, emptying, carrying objects
6. Playing with cuddly toys, push and pull toys, some activated toys
7. Rocking in rocking boat
8. Climbing steps

9. Handling nature objects
10. Looking at books
11. Looking at the Bible
12. Looking at pictures
13. Listening to records
14. Working simple puzzles
15. Having leaders sing, read, talk, listen, laugh, encourage

IN SUMMARY

A church setting carefully planned by Nursery leaders for toddler children acknowledges the following needs of toddlers:

Some adult persons to trust
Some things to explore
Freedom to move
Experience with a limited number of children for a limited time

When these factors are present, the possibilities for a happy time at church are increased. Also, a church has offered one more opportunity for children to learn through unworded experience to love their God and neighbor.

FOR GROUP DISCUSSION

Make a chart or check list of suggestions concerning facilities for babies and toddlers, as indicated in this chapter. Add to it terms of your experience. Check the facilities in your church against the chart on page 63. An approach like this might be helpful for study:

Desired Facility	What We Have	An Improvement We Could Make	How? Who? When?

CHAPTER 6

6

Birthdays Seem Important

SOMEWHERE between the chronological years of two-and-one-half and three, the growing child begins to distinguish himself in ways not previously noticed. Interested adults often acknowledge this fact with "He's not a baby anymore." And a child approaching three years of age seems to take delight in trying to display three fingers—the sign of "how many I am going to be."

I. SOME OBVIOUS GROWTH

1. *His motor co-ordination is smoother.*—The growing child's legs are getting longer. He loses his baby roly-polyness and its accompanying tumbles. He moves from what seemed a complicated process of motor control to an apparently effortless use of his body. Increasingly he climbs, carries, and manipulates with hands and feet as he desires.

2. *His language facility is extended.*—His vocabulary increases and his verbal communications include sentences. He asks and answers questions, wonders, and tells. Perhaps this increasing ability for speech more than any other accomplishment of young childhood is considered by adults as a sign of joining the human race.

3. *His activities are increasingly purposeful.*—Whereas a two-year-old shovels dirt and sand for the sake of activity and experimentation, an older three-year-old digs for a reason. In similar fashion, a three-year-old rides the

trike to go somewhere and loads the wagon with something which he names.

4. *Such purposeful play is quite logically attended by a longer attention span and imaginative, imitative play.*— "I'll be the mommy; you be the baby," says the three. Later, as he is impressed by an ever-enlarging world, the roles of fireman, policeman, and teacher come into full recognition.

As concerns home-play it should be noted that sex roles are not clearly defined at this early level. Girls can be daddies or baby brothers as readily as can boys. An observer also notes that children tire easily of one role and change quickly from "Mother" to "Baby."

5. *His social interests increase.*—People are important. A three-year-old wants to be with them even though he retains his awe of them in initial encounters. He plays cozily with another child temporarily but may leave him without warning for a more interesting companion or activity.

Of course, the companionship may come soon to an untimely end because of disagreement. Moreover, if three is not a crowd in the beginning, it will be before long. The presence of more than two children in a social setting is a clue to a trained teacher; she stays near and "moves in" knowing full well that what seems like peace cannot last very long.

II. Some Distinctive "Tasks"?

Despite obvious signs of development, this period of early childhood does not lend itself readily to a distinctive psychological summary of a "task" to perform. Infancy seems to be concerned with learning to trust the surrounding environment; toddlerhood appears to be both seeking and developing self-awareness and self-trust.

The development that comes at around three, four, and five is attended perhaps by a continuation rather than by some new distinguishing characteristic. It is as though all of the "firsts" had happened. If there is a unique quality about this period, perhaps it is found in the possibility that a child begins a slow process of finding his place in humanity at large. He takes what he has and moves on.

This is not to say that life has ceased to be exciting. Adventure is the very warp and woof of early childhood. New horizons are always just ahead. Asking questions and seeking answers is an attitude of daily living when one is three years old.

III. Some Possible Problems

Can delightful, spontaneous three-year-olds have problems? And can these charming little ones possibly *be* problems to grownups who look with envy at their energy and boundlessness?

Perhaps if all persons concerned always felt well and free from strain, the answer might be *no*. But such a state of affairs is only occasional. For the most part, three-year-olds, like their elders, must face the stern realities of every day: "I'm afraid"; "Do you like me?"; "I don't want to"; "I can't"; "I must."

When a careful observer sums up his watchfulness of three-year-olds, he is inclined to admit that they have problems and defines them thus: *Too much, too soon, for too long.*

Watch a three-year-old who is sturdily built and physically daring as he enters an unfamiliar situation to stay without his mother. He is threatened by the fact that his mother plans to leave him. He cries. Adults who have observed his physical prowess but not his emotional insecurity rebuke him: "Oh you're not going to cry? You're a *big* boy; big boys don't cry." This is *too much, too soon*. He is *not* a big boy. He is a three-year-old who is having his first experience with separation. He has not had much practice with emotional control. He will need time for growth in this area.

Another three, an only child who has had few social experiences except with adults, is thrust into the midst of a vigorous, shrill group of Nursery-age children. She is urged to "go play." She draws back, resists, and insists upon going home. *Too much, too soon.* Here, likewise, patient waiting for security to come is in order for the child.

A sensitive, play-alone three whose frustration level is low is forced by circumstances to be in a group for all day. For two hours he manages fairly well. After that he screams and hits and bites. *Too much, too long.* A shorter day with fewer children and more occasions to be by himself even in the group may reduce the tensions of *too much, too long*.

An eager-to-please, I-have-much-to-tell three begins to stutter. On other occasions, he may drop objects or stumble awkwardly. *Just too much.*

Three-year-olds must face reality—yes. But can one expect of them the same degree of acceptance and fortitude which adults are able to muster? Does not the fact of having been in the world only three years merit sympathy and patient waiting for the security which can come only with experience?

The three-year-old knows the eternal struggle of independence-dependence and security-freedom. His parents and friends may help him face his enlarging world by giving him time, sympathy, and personal behavior worthy of imitation.

IV. Some Opportunities of Religious Significance

In the light of some of the facts and feelings which friendly adults have about three-year-olds, a question is raised. What are some experiences of religious significance to this age level? How may such experiences be nurtured and not hindered? What can the church offer to persons three years old? The following ideas are given as suggestions for thought and action among persons who are eager to share the Christian message with young children.

1. *To live with adults who acknowledge God and commit themselves to him in faith may be an experience of religious significance for three-year-olds.*—This point of catching attitudes and action from adults has been made repeatedly in preceding pages about infancy and toddlerhood. This remains the most important fact in the continuing experience of early childhood. To see persons in quiet meditation and prayer; to hear unstrained, thoughtful religious conversation; to feel sympathy extended toward someone who has done wrong; to witness reconciliation between one who asks forgiveness and one who forgives—these overtones of religious living are absorbed by a sensitive, seeking three-year-old and perhaps used by him in later conscious experience.

2. *To be exposed to a larger world of wonder in the presence of a reverent adult can be a meaningful experience of religious significance to a three-year-old.*—Such times are not always accompanied by words. The nonverbal expressions of awe and wonder are just as often told with eyes and hands. Nor is reverence always quiet in its expression. The family driving in the late afternoon sunset may suddenly become excitedly aware of the ball of fire and of the blaze of colors across the sky. In a quite

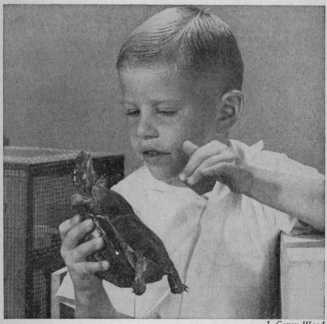

J. Carey Wood

"To be exposed to a larger world of wonder in the presence of a reverent adult can be a meaningful experience of religious significance to a three-year-old."

Robert Jackson

"Through play, persons are valued as individuals; each one can be himself; each person can do something different from others."

different way the young child may experience reverence in wonder as he stands close to his daddy and observes a new baby sister.

3. *To have honest answers to honest questions furthers the religious quest.*—"What's in my head?" "Where was I when you were born?" To the startled adult, the questions seem more easily raised than answered. But there must be no evading, no putting off, no make-believe, no saying, "I don't know," if the adult does know. The reply may be simple; it may be sufficient; the child himself is the judge.

4. *To receive and share ideas which reveal faith without dogmatism leaves the way open for further religious*

wondering and experiencing.—To hear positive answers stated in precisely worded symbolic phrases puts an end to reflection and communion. To sense faith keeps a way open. "We don't know all the reasons; we want to know more and more. We know God is good; he will help us find better answers."

5. *To have adults recognize the importance of play furthers the possibilities for religious growth.*—Through play, persons are valued as individuals; each one can be himself; each person can do something different from all others.

The timid and unvalued child can be recognized and encouraged. In play, awareness of other persons as important is inevitable. Likewise, through play, creativity which is God-given is preserved and nurtured for worship and work.

6. *To be able to join a group in a church setting where these possibilities of religious significance are recognized is an experience of positive religious value for most three-year-olds.*—Not all children of this age are ready for group situations. Neither are all group situations in church settings of positive religious value. (See chapter 8 for suggestions about evaluating groups.) Where the factors of readiness to belong and readiness to receive are mutual, the potential for increased awareness of God and neighbor is high.

FOR GROUP DISCUSSION

1. Observe a three-year-old child carefully for a period of at least forty-five minutes or more. What did his behavior tell you about him?
2. List some problems of a three-year-old you have observed. Do

you have any reasonable hunches about their cause? Any ideas about how these burdens might be lessened for this three-year-old?

3. Observe three-year-old children at play. What values of religious significance did you see?

4. Is your church well prepared to receive and guide three-year-olds?

CHAPTER 7

7

Away from Home

THE COMPLEXITY of today's economic, social, and organizational life compels parents of young children to answer some questions which very likely would not even have been raised two generations ago. Shall a mother work outside her home? Shall she work part time or full time? If she does work, who will care for her children?

If a mother does not work outside her home, shall the three- to five-year-old in the family attend an organized group for children anyway? Why or why not? How much shall families that have young children participate in all of the organized activities of their church and community?

Many groups attempt to give parents ready answers to these questions. Classified ads in local newspapers advertise "children kept." Announcements of meetings at the church add a general to-be-expected reminder, "nurseries open." Some department stores and restaurants now provide a free baby sitting "service" while the mothers shop.

Some parents never question these convenient arrangements. But other people, and thoughtful persons in professional groups concerned with the well-being of children, doubt the rightness of some types of group experience for young children. They continue to work for increased understanding of the effect of group experience in the life of a young child.

I. POSITIVE VALUES OF GROUPS

Some group experiences contribute positively to a child's emotional, physical, and mental growth. In carefully purposed and well-planned settings, a child around three years of age can become increasingly aware of other persons, find growing security outside his home and parents, discover satisfying ways to be with his peers, and increase his explorations and understandings of the world around him.

II. NEGATIVE EFFECTS OF GROUPS

On the other hand, many group experiences affect a child's growth negatively. In them and because of them he becomes frightened, rebellious, high-strung, and noncommunicative. In poor group settings—including those to be found in churches—a child is exposed frequently to disease, to uncleanliness, and to physical dangers, all of which can accompany overcrowding and understaffing.

Unfortunately, far too many parents give little thought to discovering the positive or negative effects of particular group experiences either in the church environment or in weekday situations. Whatever group is the closest and will keep the most or the longest for the least money or effort on the parents' part is all too frequently chosen by them.

III. SOME QUESTIONS TO RAISE

Increasingly, however, thoughtful parents are giving attention to the effects of a child's relationships outside his home. They are asking: When is he ready to be introduced to a group? Under what conditions? Where can one find appropriate first experiences outside our home? Which church in our town seems most adequately prepared to minister to young children in Sunday group settings?

IV. THE MINISTRY OF A CHURCH TO YOUNG CHILDREN IN GROUPS

A church which allows and encourages the attendance of young children in its organized activities is responsible for evaluating these settings. It is not valid to presume that the experiences which children have are necessarily good just because they are happening in the church building. It is very possible in some situations that the children are receiving more negative than positive learning.

Likewise, a church is responsible for acknowledging that learning of religious significance comes also to the children in groups outside the church environment. As the young child finds trust or mistrust with many persons and places outside his home, he is having experiences of religious significance. He is developing an emotional attitude which may help or hinder his finding God trustworthy.

Thus, in its broader ministry, a church extends its care for young children when it expresses concern for the well-being of children in groups outside the church setting. Persons who preach love and the worth of the individual cannot remain silent when children are herded together in inadequate space and with too few adults.

Nor can caring persons avoid voting for the legal protection of children in groups through properly licensed child-care facilities.

V. SOME WAYS TO JUDGE GROUP SETTINGS

Whether the group is one of the many which a church sets up in its organized·life, or a public or private nursery school or day care center, these general areas of evaluation are important to consider.

THE PLACE

1. Does it look as if it is planned for the well-being of children, or is it arranged mostly for the convenience of adults?

2. To what extent does it acknowledge children's needs for activity-space?

3. Is it clean, scrubbed, dry, bright?

4. Are there adequate toileting facilities? If so, where?

5. Is there sanitary, convenient facility for drinking water?

6. Is there approved fire inspection? Protection from other safety threats?

7. Is there provision for safe, active, varied outdoor play?

THE PERSONS (Adults)

1. Do they seem to enjoy children? Do they have warmth and spontaneity?

2. What kind of experience and training have they had? What kind of attitude do they have toward further learning?

3. Are they emotionally mature? For example, how

would they respond to a child with a tantrum? a storm? an invasion by an irrational person?

4. Are they physically able to endure the strain of caring for children?

5. Are they able to relate to parents as well as to children?

6. Can they keep confidences?

7. Are they worthy of imitation?

THE PLAN

1. Is there a maximum limit for enrolment in keeping with space and personnel and age level requirements of the children?

2. Are there sufficient numbers of adults to maintain a ratio of one adult to four or five children?

3. Do the adults in charge seem to have a clear idea of their purpose? Are these purposes written or oral or both?

4. Does the program fit the development level of the child? Does the program allow for freedom of movement, creative response, variety in activities, and some flexibility?

5. Are all children treated alike or is there acknowledgment that each child is an individual?

6. Is behavior labeled good or bad and treated by specific punishment, or is thought given to the reasons for a child's response?

7. What is the attitude toward discipline? Do adults believe that discipline means teaching children merely to obey and to submit, or do they believe it is helping children to evaluate, to understand, and to live within limits?

8. How is a child's growth encouraged and evaluated —by competition and comparison with other children or in terms of himself?

9. Is there any plan for a child's gradual introduction to the group in the church, or is he simply brought and left?

10. Are there any limitations regarding health and illness—for both teachers and children?

11. Is there any plan for the exchange of ideas between parents and teachers?

12. Finally, if this is a weekday situation, is it licensed by some state agency? If it is a Sunday setting, would it pass all of the minimum standards set up by a state agency?

Are the persons involved—parents, volunteer teachers, or teachers receiving pay—willing to have such an evaluation and act in the light of the findings?

Many churches in their organized programs are providing maximum learning opportunities for their young children. They have worked to have devoted personnel, adequate meeting places, good equipment, and a purposeful program. Some of these churches are providing good weekday facilities for young children also. The fact that many churches have met the challenge of young children in these ways can be an inspiration to other churches for a more courageous evaluation of their own responsibilities.

FOR GROUP DISCUSSION

1. What is the adult-child ratio in the group settings of church or community or private facilities you know?
2. What are the minimum requirements in your state for licensing child-care facilities?

3. In the light of suggestions in this chapter, re-examine your responsibility as a parent, as a church member, and as a community participant.

CHAPTER 8

8

Too Much for You?

SOME CONSIDERATION OF PROBLEMS

FOR the most part, life with children goes along in a to-be-expected pattern of balance between tears and laughter, ups and downs. But not infrequently there sometimes appears a noticeable imbalance. The once-happy child cries more than he has before; he whines; he becomes excessively demanding; he has bladder or bowel "accidents." Given a chance, he bullies other children. He is just "too much for me."

What to do? praise? reward? threaten? punish? shame? remind?

One action word seems more appropriate than any other as a fundamental approach and a basic continuing point of view: It is *inquire.* A concerned adult needs to ask, Why is this? What causes this sudden emotional temperature?

A thoughtful parent or teacher may be able to discover something in himself or in other people related to the child which is the cause of stress. Likewise, there may be places or things or events which offer clues to the young child's behavior.

I. SOME QUESTIONS TO ASK ABOUT PROBLEMS

1. *Is this a to-be-expected response at this level of development?*—It is not unusual for a three-year-old to have toilet accidents; it is a matter of concern when a

five-year-old continues in this pattern (or returns to it). In like manner one is not surprised when a two-year-old takes, pulls, pushes, grabs, or bites. These are rather normal beginnings of social responses; we expect two-year-olds gradually to learn better ways. One is, however, a bit more questioning when a five-year-old seems to respond consistently in only a primitive manner. As has been indicated elsewhere in this book, some so-called problems are problems only to those adults who will not recognize the factor of developmental readiness.

2. *Has there been some change in routine, person, places, things?*—Is a loved person absent—temporarily or permanently? Is a new person present—a baby, a grandparent, a neighbor, a new stepparent? Has there been a move—to another bed or room, to a new house, to a different town or church? Is the child with groups of people more frequently than he has been before?

3. *Is anything different happening in the family relationship?*—Is either parent concerned about a problem which he may or may not express in words? What are the feelings between husband and wife? between parents and other children? between siblings? Threats to security do not have to be spoken aloud to affect a young child's sense of well-being. He is equipped with a sensitive built-in barometer to emotional overtones. Though he may be too young for words himself, he responds nonetheless to the qualities in a human voice which express anger and rebellion or tenderness and sympathy. As he grows in perception, he likewise is aware of the destructive language in unfriendly silence, in withering glances, or in tight facial muscles. The child's feeling of security is threatened by any rift between his parents. Such an

occurrence seems to leave him out, to cause him to be forgotten. "Who will take care of me?" "Who will give me approval and affection if these nearest to me seem not to show it for one another?" A child is tense or relaxed in direct relation to the similar state in his parents or in his temporary parents.

4. *Is more being expected of the child than he can give?*—A child is sometimes more "grown" in one area than in another and this fact can be to his disadvantage. For example, a child may be unusually able and mature physically—"big for his age." Unless adults are very careful, they will expect performance in every area to be equally mature. Can a two-year-old eat without making a mess? Should a three-year-old be expected to sit quietly? Is a five-year-old ready for formal schooling? Can young children understand the symbolism of many Bible stories?

5. *What is his physical condition?*—Does he have abundant energy? Is he sleeping well? Does he eat well? Has he had a recent illness?

Sometimes even the most searching analysis on the part of devoted parents fails to reveal needed insights. Here it is that our present-day world offers help beyond that of two generations ago. Knowledge of human growth and development and behavior is fast-growing; desire to share its values is widespread; help with the problems of children and their families is almost as near as the telephone.

II. THE MINISTER AS COUNSELOR

The Christian minister is a messenger of love and reconciliation; he wants to be helpful to families in times of crises. Very often he is able to lead concerned persons to think anew about a barren situation and to find ways of changing it. On the other hand, the minister often recognizes that the person needs professional counsel and more help than the time of his total ministry will allow him. Here again, the present-day minister is acquainted with the facilities for helping children and families of his community and the larger community. He can refer persons to these agencies.

For some people the quickest way to ease mounting tension is to consult the family physician, a psychologist, a psychiatrist, or a professional counselor. For others the sometimes-less-quick but equally competent help of community agencies is an adequate answer to pressing needs. The person one seeks for help is important but of equal importance is that one *does seek* help. "It is a sign of strength to ask for help." [1]

III. SOME COMMUNITY AGENCIES

Through state, federal, and local support, specialized help which parents (or others) need is easily available. Some services were originally offered for the benefit of persons who could not pay for professional help. This fact is no longer necessarily true of the services of many agencies.

The Public Health Department offers nursing and advisory service to those who inquire. Their help includes well-baby clinics, prenatal care for mothers, immunization clinics, orthopedic and cerebral palsy clinics for physically handicapped children, film service on health subjects, and mental hygiene and child guidance clinics.

[1] Words often used by Family Service agencies.

These two latter services are becoming increasingly prominent among community agencies. In some communities, separate agencies function to provide the services. In some localities, these services are extended to both adults and children. In other communities, agencies are concerned chiefly with the emotional problems of children and parents. Services offered usually include psychological testing and psychiatric and social counseling. Parents may be referred to the agency by their family doctor, the public school teacher, or the public health nurse. Parents must ask for an appointment.

In some states, the Public Health Department is responsible for the advising and licensing of group care facilities for young children (day care centers). In other states this important responsibility is vested in the Welfare Department of the county and state.

The Welfare Department in each county or parish is helpful in many services to children and parents. This agency guides in adoption, offers suggestions concerning neglected or orphaned children, provides foster home care during a parent's incapacity, or gives financial assistance to a dependent mother and children. In small communities, the Welfare Department perhaps can most readily put the inquiring person in touch with other agencies which offer specialized help.

The Family Service Agency and the Domestic Court are available in many communities for counseling in the area of family relationships and personal problems. In some localities, the former is especially distinctive in its homemaker service. This is a temporary help given to families otherwise unable to keep the family together and cared for at home during an emergency—such as a

mother's illness. Through counseling with a social
worker, a mother is able to secure someone to stay in the
home and to care for her family for a period of weeks.
This service is sometimes extended to other situations,
such as the illness of an elderly person.

The American Red Cross and the Veteran's Administration are helpful to servicemen and their families.

IV. PARENTS' AND CITIZENS' GROUPS

Organizations and associations for parents of exceptional children are becoming more and more prominent
in all communities. If a child seems gifted or mentally re-
tarded, if he is crippled or partially sighted or spastic or
deaf, there is very likely some specialized group of mutually interested parents and friends. These groups are organized to give help to one another and to reach out to
other parents of exceptional children. For further information about such groups, write to The Council for
Exceptional Children, NEA, 1207 16th Street, N.W.,
Washington 6, D.C.

Young children and their parents are the concern of
many people who give time, thought, energy, and money
for implementing their concern. All persons who are associated with children and parents are urged to become
familiar with the resources in the community and beyond
which can give specialized help in time of need.

FOR GROUP DISCUSSION

Ask some members of helping professions in your county or
city to tell of services available to families of young children.

Make a display or file of free literature from these agencies on
page 89:

1. Agricultural Extension Service, Cornell University, Ithaca, New York

2. Association for Childhood Education International, 3615 Wisconsin Avenue, N.W., Washington 16, D.C.

3. Bureau of Education Experiments, 69 Bank Street, New York, New York

4. Child Development Institute, Teacher's College, Columbia University, New York, New York, or Bureau of Publications, 525 West 120th Street, New York 27, New York

5. Child Study Association of America, 132 East 74th Street, New York 21, New York

6. Merrill-Palmer School, 71 East Ferry Avenue, Detroit, Michigan

7. National Association for Nursery Education, Roosevelt College, 430 South Michigan Avenue, Chicago 5, Illinois

8. National Congress of Parents and Teachers, 600 South Michigan Boulevard, Chicago 5, Illinois

9. National Association for Mental Health, 1790 Broadway, New York 19, New York

10. Play Schools Association, 1941 Broadway, New York, New York

11. U. S. Department of Agriculture, Extension Division, Bureau of Home Economics, Washington, D.C.

12. Office of Education, Superintendent of Documents, Washington 25, D.C.

13. Federal Security Agency, Children's Bureau, Washington 25, D.C.

14. Science Research Associates, 57 West Grand Avenue, Chicago 10, Illinois

15. Association for Family Living, 28 East Jackson, Chicago 4, Illinois

16. Public Affairs Committee, Inc., 22 East 38th Street, New York 16, New York

17. Committee on Mental Health, State Charities Aid Association, 105 East 22nd Street, New York, New York

18. Group Service Bureau, *Parent's Magazine*, 52 Vanderbilt Avenue, New York 17, New York

19. The Baptist Sunday School Board, 127 Ninth Avenue, North, Nashville 3, Tennessee
   Director of Nursery Work, Training Union Department
   Superintendent of Nursery Work, Sunday School Department

CHAPTER 9

9

When Adults Say Hello

GETTING ACQUAINTED WITH NURSERY CHILDREN

A PARENT and his child are walking along at a leisurely pace, exchanging ideas and making plans. They seem to be enjoying each other. In the midst of such spontaneous companionship, another person, an acquaintance of the parent, appears. The two adults greet each other in their accustomed manner. Then the acquaintance turns his attention to the child. What will happen now? Is there any parent who has not dreaded the moment of meeting between his child and a particular adult? And in contrast, has not the appearance of another adult brought joy to both parent and child? What factors make the difference between pleasure and discomfort? How does an adult's approach to children affect the possibilities for continuing or ending a desired relationship?

I. SOME USUAL WAYS TO SAY HELLO

Some good-natured persons meet children with teasing: "That's a fine *boy* you have there" (despite the obvious hair ribbons and pink dress which a little girl is wearing). Or, "Say, I just saw a policeman; he told me that he was looking for your daddy."

Some adults will gush; still others will punch or tickle or boo. And many will ask the inevitable question, How old are you?

Sometimes a less threatening form of introduction is

made to children. A warmhearted person offers candy or gum; another takes something of interest out of his pocket; still another may try a friendly pat.

II. SOME USUAL RESPONSES

Children's reactions vary. Frequently they remain shyly quiet or hide their faces against the security of the parent's body. The more experienced ones may resist teasing and physical approaches with cautious attempts at hitting back or sticking out their tongues. Less daring ones become sullen and make persistent loud efforts to pull their parents away from this intrusion. Some children anticipate the nature of an encounter when they see particular people and parents: "Don't let Mr. M———— get me!"

These meetings of friend and child are equally hard on parents. The struggle between pride in the "acceptable" behavior of one's child and sympathy with him is difficult to resolve happily for all concerned. Some parents settle immediately for the approval of friends: "Say hello to Mr. B————." Other parents make efforts to interpret to children the well-meaning intentions of the strange-acting adult: "Mr. B———— likes you. He is teasing you." The frequency or infrequency of such encounters may enable a parent to decide what his policy of response will be.

III. THE CHILD DEVELOPMENT WAY

In previous chapters this book has sought to describe the nature and needs of Nursery children in terms of progressive growth and development. Questions have been raised: What are Nursery children like? What are they trying to do? What problems does their striving bring to themselves and to others? When are they ready for change?

In this chapter it is appropriate to recall some basic ideas suggested in an effort to answer yet other questions: How does one initiate and maintain a pleasant personal friendliness with young children? In the light of what is known about the growth and development of Nursery children, what is a good way to say hello? How can an adult introduce himself to a person who is one, two, or three years old?

In the following paragraphs, some previously stated basic facts are recalled and subsequent clues to developing friendliness with young children are briefly discussed.

Children are persons—each different from all others. Personhood is not synonymous with adulthood; it is equally the right of infancy. In this point of view is found the most important clue to developing friendliness with children: *Value children as important people worthy of the same degree of respect and reticence one would give an adult person.*

Seen as persons, children are no longer playthings or objects for adult amusement. They are made in the image of God and are to be valued as his creation.

Young children are learning to trust. They are cautiously reaching out to find security and dependability in the world around them. For those who seek friendliness this fact demands: *Be trustworthy.*

This is not an appropriate age for teasing or magic or half-truth. One must be honest, factual, and consistent.

Children's experiences with word-language and with

reasoning are just beginning. They want to say and know more; they will in time. For the present, adults must remember: *Speak simply and avoid complicated questions*.

Nursery children find meaning in unworded experiences. They are often content to watch in contemplative quietness. This fact should be a reminder to adults: *Enjoy and value silent companionship*. For a change, try talking only when children want to talk.

Young children learn through sensory experiences and explorations—touching, tasting, looking, listening. This is how the world of people and things becomes meaningful. The clue for developing friendliness? *Be prepared for exploration—of one's self and of one's belongings!*

Nursery children who are well physically are active. This is one of nature's demands. For adults who want to be liked this means: *Accept and allow for as much activity as possible*.

Do not attempt to hold a child for long or be disappointed at his insistence upon being mobile.

Nursery children need and expect some restrictions. This is a part of seeking order and dependability. For friends of children this means: *Be fair, consistent, and firm in enforcing necessary limitations*.

Young children are increasingly aware of people but they have comparatively few experiences with strangers. The clue to approach: *Move slowly; take time; wait*.

Listen to Nan as she voices her feelings: "I don't like faces that are crossish; I don't like people that are rushy. I like medium quick ones—half slow."[1]

Nursery children move from one level of readiness to

---

[1] Dorothy Walker Baruch, *Parents and Children Go to School*. (Atlanta: Scott, Foresman and Co., 1939), p. 296.

another. They are able to participate, to enjoy, or to understand only as they are ready physically, emotionally, or mentally. The potential friend of children follows this practice: *Think about the developmental level of this person.* What is he ready for and thereby interested in? Is he ready for words? for a still object? a moving object? a game? magic? riddles? conversation about pets?

Nursery children are increasingly interested in the world of people, but they must find out about them in their own good time and way. Despite parents' urgings to "say hello," a Nursery child may not be able to extend this greeting. Adults who want to be his friends can help him to spontaneous friendliness—which may or may not use words for expression. The child himself gives the clues to readiness. The adult's part is to value, to enjoy, to accept, to allow, and to think. Then one day, because an adult has listened and watched and waited, the face of a child lights up. Without words, the two have spoken. Adult and child have said HELLO!

FOR GROUP DISCUSSION

1. Can one say hello to a child without speaking?
2. Make a list of activities or materials or interest questions which you might offer a child visiting in your home.
3. What could you offer to a three-year-old for whom you had unexpectedly become responsible during an emergency?

Selected Readings
About Young Children

GENERAL TEXTS ON HUMAN DEVELOPMENT

Jenkins, Gladys G., and others. *These Are Your Children*. (Expanded edition.) Illinois: (Scott) A. Whitman, 1953.

Jersild, Arthur T. *Child Psychology*. (Fifth edition.) Englewood Cliffs, New Jersey: Prentice-Hall, Inc., 1960.

Stone, L. Joseph, and Church, Joseph. *Childhood and Adolescence: A Psychology of the Growing Person*. New York: Random House, 1957.

EMPHASIS ON INFANCY

Aldrich, C. Anderson, and Mary M. *Babies Are Human Beings*. (Second edition, paperback available.) New York: Macmillan Co., 1954.

Ribble, Margaret A. *The Rights of Infants*. New York: Columbia University Press, 1943.

Spock, Benjamin. *The Common Sense Book of Baby and Child Care*. New York: Duell, Sloan, & Pearce, 1946.

————. *Baby and Child Care*. New York: Pocket Books, Inc., 1946.

————, and Reinhart, John. *A Baby's First Year*. New York: Duell, Sloan, & Pearce, 1955.

EMPHASIS ON EARLY CHILDHOOD

Baruch, Dorothy W. *Understanding Young Children*. New York: Bureau of Publications, Teacher's College, Columbia University, 1949.

————. *New Ways in Discipline*. New York: McGraw-Hill Book Co., Inc., 1949.

————. *How to Discipline Your Children*. Pamphlet No. 154, New York: Public Affairs Committee, 1955.

Spock, Benjamin. *Dr. Spock Talks with Mothers*. The Riverside Press, Cambridge, 1961.

Burgess, Helen Steers. *Discipline, What Is It?* New York: Child Study Association, 1938.

Fraiberg, Selma H. *The Magic Years*. New York: Charles Scribner's Sons, 1959.

Hartley, Ruth E., Frank, Lawrence K., and Goldenson, Robert M. *Understanding Children's Play*. New York: Columbia University Press, 1952.

Hymes, James L., Jr. *A Child Development Point of View*. New York: Prentice-Hall, Inc., 1955.

————. *The Child Under Six*. Washington: Educational Services, 1961.

Ilg, Frances L., and Ames, Louise B. *Child Behavior*. New York: Harper, 1955.

Preston, George H. *The Substance of Mental Health*. New York: Rinehart, 1943.

Redl, Fritz. *Understanding Children's Behavior*. New York: Bureau of Publications, Teacher's College, Columbia University Press, 1949.

Ribble, Margaret A. *Personality of the Young Child*. Columbia University Press, 1955.

Woodcock, Louise P. *Life and Ways of the Two-Year-Old*. New York: Basic Books, Inc., 1941.

Faegre, Marion L. *Your Child from One to Six*. Prepared by Mrs. Faegre, under supervision of Dr. Katherine Bain. Washington: Children's Bureau, U.S. Dept. of Health, Education, and Welfare. Publication No. 30. 1956. (Revised)

EMPHASIS ON FAMILY RELATIONSHIPS

Bossard, James H. S. *Ritual in Family Living*. Philadelphia: University of Pennsylvania Press, 1950.

Hymes, James L., Jr. *Being a Good Parent*. New York: Bureau of Publications, Teacher's College, Columbia University, 1949.

————. *Understanding Your Child*. New York: Prentice-Hall, Inc., 1952.

PAMPHLETS

Auerbach, Aline B. *How to Give Your Child a Good Start*. New York: Child Study Association of America, 1951.

Grossman, Jean Schick. *You Don't Have to Be Perfect* (even if you are a parent). New York: National Association of Mental Health, 1948.

Neisser, Walter and Edith. *Making the Grade as Dad*. Pamphlet No. 157. New York: Public Affairs Committee, 1955.

Wolf, Anna W. M. *What Makes a Good Home: The Beginnings of Emotional Growth*. New York: Child Study Association of America, 1951.

Hymes, James L., Jr. *Enjoy Your Child—Ages 1, 2, and 3.* Pamphlet No. 141. New York: Public Affairs Committee, 1955.

Thompson, William T. *Adventures in Parenthood.* Richmond: John Knox Press, 1959.

EMPHASIS ON GROUP EXPERIENCE

Barnouw, Else, and Swan, Arthur. *Adventures with Children.* (In nursery school and kindergarten.) New York: Thomas Crowell Co., 1959.

Christianson, Helen M., and others. *The Nursery School: Adventure in Living and Learning.* Boston: Houghton Mifflin Co., 1961.

Havighurst, R. J. *Developmental Tasks and Education.* (Second edition.) New York: Longmans, 1952.

Heffernan, Helen, ed. *Guiding the Young Child.* (Second edition.) Boston: D.C. Heath & Co., 1959.

Langford, Louise M. *Guidance of the Young Child.* New York: Wiley, 1960.

Moore, Sallie Beth, and Richards, Phyllis. *Teaching in the Nursery School.* New York: Harper & Brothers, 1959.

Moustakas, Clark E., and Berson, Minnie P. *The Young Child in School.* New York: Whiteside, Inc., and William Morrow & Co., 1956.

Moustakas, Clark E. *The Teacher and the Child.* New York: McGraw-Hill Book Co., 1956.

Read, Katherine H. *The Nursery School.* (Third edition.) A Human Relations Laboratory. Philadelphia: W. B. Saunders & Co., 1960.

Rudolph, Marguerita. *Living and Learning in the Nursery School.* New York: Harper, 1955.

EMPHASIS ON RELIGIOUS LEARNING

Anderson, Phoebe M. *Religious Living with Nursery Children.* Boston: Pilgrim Press, 1956.

_____. *3's in the Christian Community.* Boston: United Church Press, 1960.

Bro, Margueritte H. *When Children Ask.* (Revised edition.) New York: Harper, 1956.

Campbell, Elizabeth W. *Security for Young Children.* Chicago: Pilgrim Press, 1952.

Dillard, Polly Hargis. *Improving Nursery Departments.* Nashville: Convention Press, 1959.

Fahs, Sophia L. *Today's Children and Yesterday's Heritage.* Boston: Beacon Press, 1954.

Haxton, Jennie N. *When the Two-Year-Old Comes to Church.* Nashville: Graded Press, 1950.

Howe, Ruel L. *Man's Need and God's Action.* Greenwich, Conn.: Seabury Press, Inc., 1953.

Manwell, Elizabeth, and Fahs, Sophia L. *Consider the Children: How They Grow.* (Revised edition.) Boston: Beacon Press, 1951.

Miller, Randolph Crump. *Biblical Theology and Christian Education.* New York: Charles Scribner's Sons, 1956.

Sherrill, Lewis Joseph. *The Opening Doors of Childhood.* (Seventh printing.) New York: Macmillan Co., 1950.

_____. *The Struggle of the Soul.* New York: Macmillan Co., 1951.

_____. *Gift of Power.* New York: Macmillan Co., 1955.

Smart, James D. *The Teaching Ministry of the Church.* Philadelphia: Westminster Press, 1954.

Thompson, Jean A., and others. *Before They Are Three* (Infants and two-year-olds in home and church.) Philadelphia: Westminster Press, 1954.

Zimmerman, Eleanor. *Now We Are Three.* Philadelphia: Muhlenberg Press, 1960.

Suggestions for the Teacher

WHO WILL LEAD IN THIS STUDY

THE SECTION "For Group Discussion" at the close of each chapter is meant to give the teacher ideas for leadership. In addition, the following ideas are offered as possibilities for enriching the study.

1. While introducing the study, suggest that persons probably came to the group with specific questions. Ask members to list these questions (without signatures if they desire) and give them to you. Your awareness of the question will give you some ideas about the experiences and interests of the group you are teaching. Likewise, the class members' participation in such listing should give a beginning sense of direction to their study. Share the listing with the class members.

An alternate way to secure the listing is through the use of buzz groups. Divide the class into groups of four or five members. Ask each group to compile a list of questions pertinent for class discussion. Let each group report on its list of questions.

2. Perhaps the members of some church represented in the class will work with you in presenting an analysis of their church situation in the manner suggested in "For Group Discussion," chapter 5. Or, if there are enough key people to be group leaders, one session might be given to a laboratory period in which several groups from the churches represented analyze their settings and report findings of special significance to the entire group.

3. Plan for a laboratory session in which small groups evaluate resource literature (pp. 96–99) in terms of its appropriateness for designated age-group levels of development. Lead questions might be: Does this seem right for particular children I know and work with? Why or why not?

4. In another session suggest that members make pieces of equipment or material appropriate to a particular age level of development. Ideas might be: a piece of clothing, a toy, a story, a song. Persons should be able to justify their design. Encourage creative ideas.

5. Make assignments for study and summary reports on problems of particular concern to parents of young children. Some subjects might be: thumbsucking, headknocking, toilet training, fears, failure to talk.

6. Have some professional persons from your community talk with the group about a subject of concern. Consider a nursery school supervisor, a pediatrician, a psychiatrist, a social worker.

7. If you are in an area which affords community help for the establishment of day care centers, ask a representative to tell the class of the work and to suggest ways in which concerned persons might help to foster good care for children in the community.

8. Have a display of easy-to-read bulletins and pamphlets for browsing.

9. Use an association test at some point in the discussions about the feelings of children. Ask the class members to jot down the first word or image which flicks across their minds when you say a word or phrase. Some ideas for word-calling might be: baby, diaper, crying, back-talk, Grandmother, a nursery, Sunday. Discuss common responses and their significance to these words but do not insist that class members share their list unless they wish to. The value of such an exercise is probably self-revealing to the participants.

10. At the close of the study raise these questions: Have you found some answers to some of the questions you raised at the beginning of this class? Do you have new questions or problems? Do you have ideas about finding some answers to these?

For Review and Written Work

Chapter 1

1. Make your own definition of developmental task.
2. Give some examples of "inner urge to grow." (Discussed on p. 3.)

Chapter 2

3. Try to make a sequence of growth pattern for some ability or behavior you have noticed in all children. (See pp. 12–17.)

Chapter 3

4. How would you make the following directions positive: "Don't run in the hall"; "Don't ride your trike on the grass"; "Don't go out without your coat"; "Don't put your feet on the sofa."?
5. If you are the parent of a toddler, do you have any new ideas about how you might respond to his self-assertiveness?

Chapter 4

6. Write a word picture description of a two-year-old you know.

Chapter 5

7. If you are responsible for a group of toddlers, discuss how your understanding of motor ability at this level will affect your planning for them.
8. In a similar analysis, how does your understanding of the language development of a toddler affect what you plan to offer him? Likewise, how will you be governed by the toddler's degree of social awareness?
9. What might be some ways to reduce the physical problems attached to supervising a toddler?

Chapter 6

10. How could you be a good hostess to a two-year-old who might visit in your home?

Chapter 7

11. Look at materials for two-year-olds in *Church Nursery Guide*. Think of your group of two-year-olds by name. Which of

the activities suggested do you think each will respond to best? Why?

12. In consideration of the suggestions about planning for a separate group of two's in a church setting (pp. 78 ff.), what additions and subtractions would you make in your own church?

13. When do teachers and parents "teach" two-year-olds?

Chapter 8

14. By what criteria would you measure a child's readiness to be in a group setting such as is available in the church or in the community?

Chapter 9

15. Sometimes people say, "I treat all children alike." Why do you think this approach is poor philosophy in terms of child development?

IDEAS

Jot down questions or ideas that arise as you study this book.

Discuss the questions as you participate in the group study of the book.

Or, send the questions to the Nursery editors of the Sunday School or Training Union departments, Baptist Sunday School Board, 127 Ninth Avenue North, Nashville, Tennessee 37203.

You may want to paste some pictures of children in your department or home. Under each picture note briefly ways in which this book has helped you to better understand each child.

Date Due

FEB 8 1967			